Crisis, Debt, and Default

Philip Ernstberger

Crisis, Debt, and Default

The Effects of Time Preference, Information, and Coordination

Springer Gabler

Philip Ernstberger
Frankfurt am Main, Deutschland

Dissertation Universität Trier, Fachbereich IV, 2014

ISBN 978-3-658-13230-9 ISBN 978-3-658-13231-6 (eBook)
DOI 10.1007/978-3-658-13231-6

Library of Congress Control Number: 2016935198

Printed on acid-free paper

This Springer Gabler imprint is published by Springer Nature
The registered company is Springer Fachmedien Wiesbaden GmbH

When I heard the learn'd astronomer,
When the proofs, the figures, were ranged in columns before me,
When I was shown the charts and diagrams, to add, divide,
and measure them,
When I sitting heard the astronomer where he lectured with
much applause in the lecture-room,
How soon unaccountable I became tired and sick,
Till rising and gliding out I wander'd off by myself,
In the mystical moist night-air, and from time to time,
Look'd up in perfect silence at the stars.

Walt Whitman 1865, Leaves of Grass

The effort of the economist is to see, to picture the interplay of economic elements. [...] The economic world is a misty region. [...] Mathematics is the lantern by which what before was dimly visible now looms up in firm, bold outlines.

Irving Fisher 1892, Mathematical Investigation in the Theory of Value and Price

Contents

List of Figures

Preface

In the subprime crisis we saw how bad incentives and high time preference led to behavior that increased risks that finally burst into a price drop in various asset classes. This decline in value led to defaults in the banking sector and subsequently in the industry that was hit by tightening capital markets. The crisis then spread to governments which came under pressure when granting the liabilities of the banks. With governments becoming heavily indebted also currencies came under pressure.

The relations between mortgage brokers, banks, rating agencies, and investors led to increasing risk taking since behavior was detached from accountability. In the first part of the last decade, abundant capital from expansionary policy by the central banks as well as from current account surpluses was disposable for investment opportunities. Modern financial products promised a decent return with low risk. This products combined e.g. mortgage loans to portfolios, so called Collateralized Debt Obligations (CDOs). The CDOs were scaled by seniority, received a rating and were then sold to investors. The banks could thereby reduce their liabilities on their balance sheets, which enabled them to issue more loans. Hence, banks had a strong incentive to grant more mortgages, while the risk was mainly passed to the buyers of the CDOs. The mortgage broker received a commission for every house sold. With the banks granting the loans the incentive of the broker was to sell as many houses as possible. The risk of foreclosure was handed over. The rating agencies also played a major role. The pooling of mortgages allowed to reduce the risk significantly. Consequently, the senior tranches received high ratings which made them available for a large group of institutional investors. Hence, every actor profited. The mortgage brokers, the banks, and the rating agencies all had higher sales which increased their fees. The problem was that no one was accountable for the risk.

Problems emerged when interest rates began to rise. Then the payments on mortgages increased and some lenders weren't able to pay and hence foreclosed. The houses were then put up for sale, the supply increased and prices fell. Consequently, people owning a house whose mortgage exceeded the actual value had an incentive to also foreclose, increasing the supply and the pressure on the housing market. With a higher rate of foreclosure and lower housing prices the payments to the CDOs fell which led to a price drop in the CDOs. This common risk factor emerged during the crisis but was not considered in the initial assessment of risk.

Another problem was that insurance companies and banks insured losses in CDOs through credit default swaps. Hence, a protection buyer was able to claim his loss from the bank. With cash flowing out and assets dropping simultaneously most banks had severe liquidity problems. Only interventions and emergency loans by the government prevented more defaults. Fighting a recession, governments simultaneously passed stimulus packages for the economy. With governments becoming heavily indebted pressure rose. Especially small countries with big banking sectors had severe problems. Increasing indebtedness led to capital flights from various countries that caused severe depreciations, as in the case of Iceland. Inside the EU the capital flight was illustrated by the diverging Target II balances.

The crisis showed how risk taking in certain areas can spread in a system that is strongly interconnected. While the strong interconnection and risk sharing amplifies growth and prosperity, it also amplifies risk.

In this dissertation I separately analyze different topics covering financial pathologies. The first essay deals with currency crises, in which the central bank, through setting the interest rate, steers the economy and defends against speculators. The second essay examines the effects of a rating and possible biases on the coordination of investors and the pricing of debt. The third essay uses forecasts of default probabilities and implied market default probabilities to infer the weighing of information by investors.

In the first essay we consider two actors, the central bank and speculators. The central bank is endowed with a defensive measure, e.g. the amount of reserves, and has set up a fixed exchange rate regime. Through setting the interest rate the central bank can stimulate the economy or fend off speculators. Thereby, it faces a trade-off between stimulating the economy while speculative pressure rises and defending against speculators while the economy is hampered. A regime change is associated with costs and can be forced by the state of the economy or induced by choice. In the latter case the costs for defending outweigh the costs of an immediate opt-out.

We apply an intertemporal optimization framework with endogenous exit and infinite time horizon for a system of two linear differential equations that model the evolution of the attack and the state of the fundamentals. The attack is driven by the interest rate, the fundamental state, and a herding effect. The fundamentals depend on the interest rate and a mean reversion effect.

The linear nature of the model makes a bang-bang solution optimal. Hence, the central bank can either choose an expansion or a defense policy, whereas the outcome is state dependent. In bad fundamental states, the central bank is forced to abandon the regime after the reserves are exhausted. In good states, expansion is the optimal choice, but, independent of the policy chosen, the economy necessarily evolves into an intermediate fundamental state. There, two focal points emerge to which the economy converges. Which focal point is reached depends on the time preference of the central bank. For a low time preference, the central bank is willing to bear short-term costs induced through defense to reach higher long-term fundamentals. Contrary, for a high time preference, current costs are avoided with the backdrop of lower long-term fundamentals. Therefore, we propose to take measures that lower the time preference like independence, long-term mandates, and long-term policy goals.

In the second essay, I analyze a coordination game in which investors provide the financing for a firm. Investors are endowed with the bonds and receive signals indicating the fundamental state of the firm. They receive private and public information and additionally a publicly observable rating, that can be biased. Investors process information to build a posterior belief about the fundamental state. Upon this belief investors decide whether to foreclose or to roll over. Increasing signals improve the investors' posteriors and lead to a higher rate of rollover and vice versa. Thereby the rating concentrates the beliefs of the investors and hence increases the sensitivities of the signals on the default point. The bias, if observed, reveals the exaggeration by the rating agency and leads to an equivalent adaption of beliefs. A positive bias reduces the expectations and induces more investors to foreclose.

If publicly available information improves relative to private information, multiple equilibria emerge. Thereby, the outer equilibria are stable but diverging. For infinitely precise public information or rating as well as imprecise private information, investors share the same posterior beliefs. Hence, either all investors foreclose or all investors roll over. Thereby, the fundamental state looses its impact on the equilibrium and only coordination matters.

When pricing a standardized bond with a payoff of either 1 or 0, the price forecast equals the survival probability conditional on publicly observable information. Hence, the survival probability is based on public information and the rating. I show that methods which neglect the rating's influence overprice bad debt and underprice good debt. Put differently, good borrowers have to pay a higher yield, while bad borrowers pay a lower yield if the rating is neglected in the pricing of debt. This price effect relies on the coordination effect of the rating. In case of good fundamentals, the rating increases the share of investors having favorable expectations and vice versa. Therefore, in good states, more investors roll over which increases the survival probability and the bond price based on publicly observable information. The rating allows a more accurate pricing of debt through incorporating its additional coordination effect.

A forecast of the default probability by a rating agency must therefore acknowledge the rating's own influence on the coordination of investors. Neglecting the endogeneity of the rating necessarily leads to a wrong assessment with unwanted benefits for bad borrowers and costs for good borrowers.

If a firm evolves positively and ratings are not updated continuously, then the public information signal exceeds the rating. Hence, the firm exhibits a lower posterior belief than without a rating. Consequently, the firm pays a higher risk premium, which is due to the time lag of the rating and not to underlying risk. In this context, daily assessments of risk, through market based models, provide an advantage over ratings.

In the third essay, I present a heuristic approach that relates the key variables of a coordination game with heterogenous investors to observable and computable data. This approach allows to compute the precision of public and private information.

First, I present a global game in which investors hold the bonds of a firm, as described by Morris and Shin (2004). Thereby, investors receive public and private signals and decide whether to foreclose or to roll over. I show that the global game implies two prices for the bond—a forecasted price based on public information and a market price based on public and private information. These prices depend on the weighted conditional expectations and the default point.

Second, I apply the Merton model. Considering the firm's equity as an option allows the computation of the asset value. Using the KMV extension of the Merton model, I compute the distance between the assets and the default point in standard units. This yields a forecast of the default probability of the firm.

Third, I use credit default swap spreads to derive the default probability implied by the market.

Considering a standardized bond that offers a repayment of 1 in case of success and a repayment of 0 in case of failure, the market and the forecasted price are simply the discounted survival probabilities. Connecting the signals to the computed data then allows to solve for the precision of public and private information.

An increase in the precision of public information increases the weight investors put on this information in the formation of beliefs. This leads to more homogenous beliefs that allow coordination. If public information precision is sufficiently precise relative to private information precision multiple equilibria emerge. The computation shows that private information precision increases relatively if the default probability implied by the market exceeds the forecasted default probability. In this case beliefs are more dispersed and multiple equilibria are less likely. If, however, the forecasted default probability rises and the market default probability does not follow, the precision of private information becomes imprecise. Consequently, posterior beliefs have a lower variance and multiple equilibria are more likely.

Part I.

The Dynamics of Currency Crises—Results from Intertemporal Optimization and Viscosity Solutions

Coauthor: Christian Bauer

1. Introduction

Previous literature modelling financial crises and speculative attacks highlighted particularly the aspects of speculators attacking a currency. However, it did not incorporate the main role of the central bank adequately. In fact, setting the interest rate influences the fundamentals and the costs of speculators. Thus, the behavior of the central bank is neither a passive reaction due to speculative pressure nor sole signalling—it changes the state of the economy.

If the central bank chooses to defend a fixed exchange rate regime by raising the interest rate, it accepts that fundamentals decline and furthermore accepts that the declining fundamentals reinforce the future attack and thus worsen its future position. Hence, the behavior of the central bank is crucial for both, the evolution of the economy and for its own future position. On the other hand, speculators know that attacking weakens the position of the central bank and that the attack is successful if the central bank is weak enough. Though, they also have to consider their costs if the central bank decides to defend as a reaction on the attack.

The trade-off for the central bank is that one control influences the possibility to benefit from the regime as well as the probability to bear the costs of a regime change, which occurs if the attack strength exceeds the defensive measure of the central bank.

To incorporate the trade-off, induced by the impact of the interest rate, we apply an infinite horizon intertemporal optimization framework. The time, when the central bank is forced or chooses to abandon the peg, is endogenously determined. Thus, the time horizon exceeds the duration of the regime. After briefly summarizing the literature, we first describe the general framework where we introduce the objective function and two state processes for the fundamentals and the attack. Second, we offer a solution for a simple case of the model where states are just linearly dependent on the interest rate. Third, we describe an extended linear model with fundamental feedback and herding effects.

We find that two focal points emerge, which attract the state space trajectories. A low time preference central bank will bear current costs, caused through defending, to steer the economy to the good focal point. However, a high time preference central bank avoids current losses and steers the economy to the bad focal point. Moreover, in good fundamental states with high pressure it can be optimal for the central bank to abandon the regime immediately, thereby preventing a long-term costly defense.

2. Literature

In the early models of currency crises, termed "first generation", monetizing a fiscal deficit leads to a steady decline in the reserve stock. Rational speculators anticipating the imminent exhaustion of reserves instantly withdraw their money, causing the actual crisis (cf. Krugman 1979). Flood and Garber (1984) gave an analytical solution of a Krugman type model, where arbitrary speculation can lead to a crisis. The "second generation" models speculation as a coordination problem between investors and implicitly assumes that the underlying fundamental state of the economy is common knowledge. The central bank strategically weighs the costs and benefits of a potential defense of the fixed exchange rate. Thereby, the fundamental state as well as the private expectations about a depreciation play the main role. Since private expectations alter the costs of the central bank, expectations can become self-fulfilling (cf. Obstfeld 1994 and 1996). Speculators face strategic complementarities, so that their payoffs depend on the action of others. High degrees of coordination, e.g. complete information, may result in multiple equilibria. Morris and Shin (1998) showed that if every speculator gets sufficiently precise private information, a unique equilibrium can be determined. Bauer and Herz (2013) explicitly model the strategic options of a central bank in a two stage global game. The central bank chooses its defensive measure after it observes a noisy signal about the attack strength. Thereby, it has to acknowledge the costs of defense as well as the costs for a possible devaluation. Angeletos et al. (2006) investigate the informational effects of central bank actions. Policy decisions convey information regarding the central bank's knowledge about the underlying state. This additional information allows a better coordination of speculators and produces multiple equilibria. Heinemann et al. (2004) find in experiments that global games give a good description of actual behavior. The effects of the information structure and the signals show signs in accordance with theory, but are mostly insignificant in size. This suggests that the main focus on modelling information might not be the most constructive way in approaching a better understanding of currency crises.

Morris and Shin (1999) take an approach to analyze the evolution of beliefs in a dynamic context. They investigate the changes of sentiment based on changes in the underlying fundamentals, which are assumed to follow a stochastic process. Basically, they model a sequence of repeated one shot global games, where the previous realization of the fundamentals is common knowledge. Chamley (2003) examines a dynamic global game, in which speculators utilize the movement of the exchange rate in a band as a proxy for the mass of attackers, so that it suffices as a coordination device. Predictable interventions that reduce the fluctuation in the exchange rate reduce speculator's risk and thus foster the attack. However, raising the interest rate, widening the fluctuation band, and conducting random interventions in the currency can prevent an attack. The random intervention reduces the informativeness of the exchange rate and aggravates coordination. Ceteris paribus this policy allows a smaller stock of reserves than deterministic intervention. Angeletos et al. (2007) introduce dynamics through a repeated global game, where speculators learn about the underlying fundamentals. Then, they examine equilibrium properties of different exogenous changes. Information as well as fundamentals can be the trigger for a shift from tranquility to distress. They state, without explicitly modelling, that defense is possible through higher interest rates, where the required increase depends on the quality of information of speculators about the fundamentals. Hence, defense is more costly when information improves. Guimarães (2006) introduces a Poisson process that admits a random fraction of speculators to adapt their positions. This allows to model the evolution of a crisis, where the currency can be overvalued for a long time until an attack is triggered. Admitting less speculators to change their position, raising the interest rate, or reducing the overvaluation each lower the probability of a crisis.

Nearly all approaches focus on modelling information, neglecting—particularly in dynamic setups—the crucial influence of the central bank's choice of the interest rate on the underlying fundamentals. Therefore, we present an approach that models currency crises as an intertemporal optimization problem that accounts for the reflexive nature of policy decisions. Each decision has different consequences for the future path of the economy and the future position of the central bank.

3. Model

There are two actors: the central bank and speculators. The central bank maximizes utility

$$U_0(\theta_S, A_S) = \int_0^T e^{-\rho t} u(\theta(t))\, dt + e^{-\rho T}\frac{1}{\rho} v(\theta(T) - c), \tag{1}$$

where instantaneous utility u is derived from the state of the fundamentals $\theta(t)$ and is discounted by factor ρ. The initial values of the fundamentals and the attack are $\theta_S = \theta(0)$ and $A_S = A(0)$. The overall utility U is the sum of the aggregated discounted instantaneous utility up to terminal time T plus the discounted terminal value.[1] The terminal time denotes the time when the central bank is forced to devalue and is endogenously determined by the state processes. The terminal value v is a function of the fundamentals at terminal time less an amount c representing the costs of the regime change. For the remainder of the paper, we assume that the proceeding regime is in a steady state, so that the terminal value v is constant.

The central bank maximizes the objective function (1) by setting the interest rate $r(t)$, which is always nonnegative $r(t) \geq 0$. The optimization problem is subject to the state of the system which is summarized by the state vector x that evolves according to

$$\dot{x} = \begin{pmatrix} \dot{\theta}(t) \\ \dot{A}(t) \end{pmatrix} = \begin{pmatrix} f(r(t), \theta(t)) \\ g(r(t), \theta(t), A(t)) \end{pmatrix}. \tag{2}$$

There are two state variables, the fundamentals $\theta(t)$ and the strength of the attack $A(t)$. The first state variable $\theta(t)$ enters utility directly, while the second $A(t)$ determines the terminal time $T = \inf\{t : A(t) > D\}$. This is, the first time when the strength of the attack exceeds the defensive measure D, e.g. the amount of reserves held by the central bank.[2] Hence, the central bank's control has two effects: firstly, it influences the fundamentals and thereby directly the utility. Secondly, it influences the terminal time until which utility can be accumulated and simultaneously the effect of the terminal value.[3]

[1] For the given setup $\lim_{T\to\infty} e^{-\rho T} v(\theta(T) - c) = 0$, i.e. without devaluation the second term of equation 1 vanishes.

[2] Naturally, we restrict the initial state vector to be feasible, i.e. $A(0) \leq D$.

[3] As we describe later, utility might also decrease, independent of the policy chosen, so that an early opt-out is favorable.

The change of the fundamentals depends on their own current state and the interest rate. The central bank influences the fundamentals by setting the interest rate in relation to the natural rate $\bar{r}$. For interest rates below the natural rate, the cost of credit is below the possible return on investment. As a consequence investment increases and the economic fundamentals improve and vice versa (cf. Wicksell 1898). The motion of fundamentals is often represented by a Brownian motion (cf. Morris and Shin 1999 or Guimarães 2006), where deviations of the fundamentals from the natural rate $\bar{\theta}$ tend to be reversed over time. Therefore, we define the evolution of the fundamentals by

$$\dot{\theta} = f\left(r\left(t\right), \theta\left(t\right)\right) = -f_1\left(r\left(t\right)\right) - f_2\left(\theta\left(t\right)\right). \tag{3}$$

Where $\frac{\partial f_1(.)}{\partial r(t)} > 0$ is the interest rate elasticity of the fundamentals and $\frac{\partial f_2(.)}{\partial \theta(t)} \geq 0$ is the mean reversion elasticity of the fundamentals. The mean reversion works as a stabilizing mechanism that improves bad fundamentals (below the natural level) and reduces good fundamentals (higher than the natural level). Obviously, such a fundamentals process possesses a steady state $(\theta, r) = \left(\bar{\theta}, \bar{r}\right)$ if $f_1\left(\bar{r}\right) = f_2\left(\bar{\theta}\right) = 0$.

The motion of the attack depends on the costs $r\left(t\right)$, the fundamentals $\theta\left(t\right)$, and on strategic complementarities, i.e. a herding effect $A\left(t\right)$. When speculators expect a currency to devalue, they borrow the currency and sell it against foreign money. If the devaluation takes place, the position is closed. The profit equals the amount of the devaluation minus the costs for the loan. Increasing the interest rate raises the costs for speculators causing them to refrain from attacking (cf. e.g. Angeletos et al. 2007, Chamley 2003 and Daniëls et al. 2011). Here, the interest rate has only a defensive effect if it is higher than the natural rate $\bar{r}$. Below, the attack rises due to low costs of speculation. The success of an attack depends on the fundamentals of the economy: the expected payoff of the speculators decreases when fundamentals improve (cf. Obstfeld 1996 and Morris and Shin 1998). Hence, speculators refrain from attacking if the fundamentals are above their natural rate and vice versa. However, speculators also tend to imitate the behavior of other speculators without considering their own information (cf. Banerjee 1992 and Bikhchandani et al. 1992). Due to this herding effect an increase of the attack is ceteris paribus higher if more speculators already hold positions against the currency. We treat the attack strength as a reduced form equation of the aforementioned effects. Its evolution is given by

$$\dot{A} = g\left(r\left(t\right), \theta\left(t\right), A\left(t\right)\right) = -g_1\left(r\left(t\right)\right) - g_2\left(\theta\left(t\right)\right) + g_3\left(A\left(t\right)\right), \tag{4}$$

where $\frac{\partial g_1(.)}{\partial r(t)} > 0$ is the interest rate elasticity of the attack, $\frac{\partial g_2(.)}{\partial \theta(t)} \geq 0$ is the fundamentals elasticity, and $\frac{\partial g_3(.)}{\partial A(t)} \geq 0$ is the herding elasticity. If we assume, as above, that $g_1\left(\bar{r}\right) =$

$g_2(\bar{\theta}) = 0$ and additionally that $g_3(0) = 0$ the attack is in a steady state at $(\bar{\theta}, \bar{r}, 0)$. This equals the fundamental's steady state without speculative pressure and determines a steady state of the economy.[4]

Let $V(\theta, A)$ be the value function of this optimization problem, i.e. the total utility of the central bank given it chooses an optimal control r^*

$$\begin{aligned} V(\theta_S, A_S) &= \sup_{r:[0;\infty[\to[0;\infty[} \{U_0(\theta_S, A_S)\} \\ &= U_0(\theta_S, A_S) \text{ with } \begin{pmatrix} \dot{\theta}(t) \\ \dot{A}(t) \end{pmatrix} = \begin{pmatrix} f(r^*(t), \theta(t)) \\ g(r^*(t), \theta(t), A(t)) \end{pmatrix} \\ &\qquad \text{and } \begin{pmatrix} \theta(0) \\ A(0) \end{pmatrix} = \begin{pmatrix} \theta_S \\ A_S \end{pmatrix}. \end{aligned}$$

From the value V we obtain the following Bellman equation (cf. Waelde 2008)

$$\rho V(\theta, A) = \sup_r \left\{ u(\theta) + \frac{dV(\theta, A)}{dt} \right\}. \tag{5}$$

Since V is not continuously differentiable at any feasible point,[5] a more general interpretation of this partial differential equation is necessary. As we will show, the concept of viscosity solutions applies.

3.1. Linear Version

For a first illustration of the model behavior, we set the mean reversion elasticity $\frac{\partial f_2(.)}{\partial \theta(t)}$, the fundamentals elasticity $\frac{\partial g_2(.)}{\partial \theta(t)}$, and the elasticity of herding $\frac{\partial g_3(.)}{\partial A(t)}$ equal to zero. The interest rate elasticities are assumed to be constant, where $\frac{\partial f_1(.)}{\partial r(t)} = \alpha$ and $\frac{\partial g_1(.)}{\partial r(t)} = \gamma$. With this modification, the motion of the state vector is

$$\begin{pmatrix} \dot{\theta} \\ \dot{A} \end{pmatrix} = \begin{pmatrix} -\alpha(r(t) - \bar{r}) \\ -\gamma(r(t) - \bar{r}) \end{pmatrix},$$

with $\alpha, \gamma > 0$. α is the interest rate elasticity of the fundamentals and γ the interest rate elasticity of the attack. In this simple model the central bank is confronted with a perfect correlation of fundamentals and attack. When it chooses a low interest rate to improve fundamentals, speculative pressure rises as well, and vice versa.

As a first step, we take an "educated guess" on the optimal control r^*, then show that

[4]For every state $x^* = (r^*, \theta^*, A^*)$, with $\dot{\theta}(x^*) = 0$ and $\dot{A}(x^*) = 0$, the economy is in a steady state. We will show in section 3.2.2 that the economy possesses also a steady state at maximum pressure $A = D$, in addition to no pressure $A = 0$. We call this steady states convergence or focal points.

[5]If the reserves are exhausted and a regime switch is forced, the utility jumps.

the corresponding value function indeed satisfies the Bellman equation, and finally take a closer look at the Bellman equation at the border of the state space.

The optimal control r^* depends on the state, and two cases have to be analyzed separately: the interior $A < D$ and the border case $A = D$, where any further increase in the attack would lead to a breakdown of the regime.

1. The interior case $A < D$:
   The Bellman equation is given by (cf. Waelde (2008), ch. 6; Fleming and Soner (2006), ch. 1.7)

$$\begin{aligned}\rho V(\theta, A) &= \sup_r \left\{ u(\theta) + \frac{dV(\theta, A)}{dt} \right\} \\ &= \sup_r \left\{ u(\theta) + DV \cdot \begin{pmatrix} \dot{\theta} \\ \dot{A} \end{pmatrix} \right\} \\ &= \sup_r \left\{ u(\theta) - (V_\theta \alpha + V_A \gamma)(r - \bar{r}) \right\},\end{aligned} \tag{6}$$

   with ρ as the discount factor and DV as the total derivative. The argument in the supremum is linear in r and the optimization problem (6) has a border solution $r = 0$, if and only if

$$V_\theta \alpha + V_A \gamma > 0. \tag{7}$$

   As we show later and proof in appendix 5.2.1, this condition is valid.

2. The border case $A = D$:
   The value of abandoning the regime $v(\theta - c)$ is strictly lower than the value of defending the regime $V(\theta, A = D)$ for all possible values of θ (see appendix 5.2.2). Any further increase in A would lead to an infinitely negative slope of V and is therefore avoided. Thus, the optimization problem is to maximize θ subject to $\frac{dA}{dt} \leq 0$. Since $\frac{dA}{dr} < 0$ and $\frac{d\theta}{dr} < 0$, i.e. any control increasing θ also increases A, the optimal solution is to not let A decrease. Hence,

$$r^* = \bar{r}; \quad \frac{dA}{dt} = 0; \quad \frac{d\theta}{dt} = 0. \tag{8}$$

Summarizing, the optimal control is

$$r^*(\theta, A) = \begin{cases} 0 & \text{if } A < D \\ \bar{r} & \text{else} \end{cases}.$$

Starting at an arbitrary point (θ_S, A_S), where the strength of the attack is less than the reserves $A_S < D$, the central bank maximizes the fundamentals to improve utility

(1). Therefore, the central bank conducts expansion policy, i.e. sets the interest rate to zero.[6] Hence, the fundamentals increase depending on their initial value θ_S, the interest rate elasticity α, the natural interest rate $\bar{r}$, and obviously the elapsed time t. Thus, we get as time path of the fundamentals:

$$\theta(t) = \theta_S + \int_0^t \alpha\bar{r}d\tau = \theta_S + \alpha\bar{r}t. \tag{9}$$

Expansion policy ($r(t) = 0$) reduces the costs of attacking, implying that stress increases with improving fundamentals. The attack state is a function of the initial attack level A_S, the interest rate elasticity γ, the natural interest rate $\bar{r}$, and the elapsed time t. Hence, the time path of the attack is given by:

$$A(t) = A_S + \int_0^t \gamma\bar{r}d\tau = A_S + \gamma\bar{r}t. \tag{10}$$

The optimal policy of the central bank, to set the interest rate to zero, is accompanied by increasing stress, i.e. an increasing attack. To keep the exchange rate peg, the central bank has to intervene in the currency market, i.e. to sell foreign currency. Thereby, it reduces the reserves D. Since a devaluation involves costs c that decrease the central bank's utility, it starts to defend the peg additionally through raising the interest rate in the instant before the reserves are exhausted. The time when the central bank raises the interest rate to stop speculation, but does not yet devalue, is thus denoted by $T^{A=D}$ and is called defense time, with $T^{A=D} = \min\{t : A(t) = D\}$. $T^{A=D}$ is reached, when the strength of the attack equals the reserves $A(T^{A=D}) = D$. Inserting in (10) gives the defense time

$$T^{A=D} = \frac{D - A_S}{\gamma\bar{r}}. \tag{11}$$

The central bank has to defend earlier the lower the reserves D, the higher the initial attack level A_S, the interest rate elasticity of the attack γ, and the natural interest rate $\bar{r}$ are.

When the central bank applies a restrictive monetary policy, both, stress and fundamentals stop growing and the economy is in a steady state. Therefore, we get the following

[6] As noted earlier, we require the interest rate to be nonnegative. Obviously, without this condition the optimal interest rate would be minus infinity.

time paths given the optimal control r^*

$$A(t) = \begin{cases} A_S + \gamma\bar{r}t & \text{if } t < T^{A=D} \\ D & \text{else} \end{cases}$$

$$\theta(t) = \begin{cases} \theta_S + \alpha\bar{r}t & \text{if } t < T^{A=D} \\ \theta_S + \alpha\bar{r}T^{A=D} & \text{else} \end{cases}.$$

Assuming exponential utility $u(\theta) = -\exp(-\chi\theta)$, where χ is the risk aversion parameter, the value function is:[7]

$$\begin{aligned} V &= U_0(r^*) = \\ &= -\int_0^{T^{A=D}} \exp(-\rho t)\exp(-\chi(\theta_S + \alpha\bar{r}t))\,dt \\ &\quad -\int_{T^{A=D}}^{\infty} \exp(-\rho t)\exp\left(-\chi\left(\theta_S + \alpha\bar{r}T^{A=D}\right)\right)dt \\ &= -\frac{\exp(-\chi\theta)}{\rho + \chi\alpha\bar{r}}\left(\frac{\chi\alpha\bar{r}}{\rho}\exp\left(-(\rho + \chi\alpha\bar{r})T^{A=D}\right) + 1\right). \end{aligned}$$

Now, we can show that this value function indeed solves the Bellman equation (6).[8] Rearranging and deriving with respect to the state variables θ and A delivers the costate variables V_θ and V_A

$$V_\theta = -\chi V, \quad V_A = \frac{1}{\gamma\bar{r}}\left((\rho + \chi\alpha\bar{r})V + \exp(-\chi\theta)\right).$$

The costate variables show how much a marginal increase in the respective state changes the overall value. Inserting into (7) and using the value function gives

$$\rho\left(-\frac{\exp(-\chi\theta)}{\rho + \chi\alpha\bar{r}}\left(\frac{\chi\alpha\bar{r}}{\rho}\exp\left(-(\rho + \chi\alpha\bar{r})T^{A=D}\right) + 1\right)\right) + \exp(-\chi\theta) > 0$$

which is true.[9] Hence, for the interior case $A < D$, the Bellman equation

$$\rho V(\theta, A) = \sup_r \{u(\theta) - (V_\theta\alpha + V_A\gamma)(r - \bar{r})\} \tag{12}$$

has an argument which is linear in $r(t)$ with a negative slope. Therefore, the solution to the optimization problem (6) is the minimum value of r, i.e. $r(t) = 0$.

For the border case $A = D$ we utilize the Hamiltonian notation of the problem as used in (Fleming and Soner 2006, ch. 2, lemma 8.1) and define the subsolutions D^-V

[7] A derivation of the value function and the costate variables is given in appendix 5.2.1.
[8] Inserting in the Bellman equation shows that the solution is feasible.
[9] See appendix 5.2.1.

and supersolutions D^+V. A value function belonging to both D^-V and D^+V is called a viscosity solution. For infinite horizon time-homogeneous optimization problems with discounted utility the value function takes the form $V(t,x) = \exp(-\rho t)V(x)$, where ρ is the discount factor and x the state vector (cf. Fleming and Soner 2006, ch. 1.7).

Proposition 1 *For infinite horizon time-homogeneous optimization problems with discounted utility each feasible value function is continuously differentiable with respect to the time variable t. Thus,* $\frac{\partial}{\partial t}V(t,x)$ *enters each element in* D^-V *and* D^+V *and it is sufficient to define* D^-V *and* D^+V *without the time differential.*

We now define the subsolutions D^-V and supersolutions D^+V:

$$D^+V(\theta, A) = \left\{ (p,q) \in \mathbb{R}^2 : \limsup_{\substack{(y,a)\to(\theta,A) \\ a\le D}} \frac{V(y,a) - V(\theta,A) - p(y-\theta) - q(a-A)}{\|(y,a)-(\theta,A)\|} \le 0 \right\}, \tag{13}$$

$$D^-V(\theta, A) = \left\{ (p,q) \in \mathbb{R}^2 : \liminf_{\substack{(y,a)\to(\theta,A) \\ a\le D}} \frac{V(y,a) - V(\theta,A) - p(y-\theta) - q(a-A)}{\|(y,a)-(\theta,A)\|} \ge 0 \right\}. \tag{14}$$

Since $V(\theta, A)$ is continuously differentiable in all feasible states, we have $D^+V(\theta,A) = D^-V(\theta,A) = (V_\theta(\theta,A), V_A(\theta,A))$, which solve the Bellman equation. In addition to this standard definition we also define the sub- and supersolutions from beyond the feasible state, i.e. the region of states in which the regime ends. We will apply this to the Bellman equation to include controls which might end the regime:

$$D^+_{out}V(\theta, D) = \left\{ (p,q) \in \mathbb{R}^2 : \limsup_{\substack{(y,a)\to(\theta,D) \\ a> D}} \frac{V(y,a) - V(\theta,D) - p(y-\theta) - q(a-D)}{\|(y,a)-(\theta,D)\|} \le 0 \right\}, \tag{15}$$

$$D^-_{out}V(\theta, D) = \left\{ (p,q) \in \mathbb{R}^2 : \liminf_{\substack{(y,a)\to(\theta,D) \\ a> D}} \frac{V(y,a) - V(\theta,D) - p(y-\theta) - q(a-D)}{\|(y,a)-(\theta,D)\|} \ge 0 \right\}. \tag{16}$$

Since the value after the regime change $\nu(\theta - c) = V(y,a)$ is strictly smaller than the value of remaining in the regime $V(\theta, D)$, we have $D_{out}^{+}V(\theta, D) = \{(p,q) \in \mathbb{R}^2 : \limsup \mathbb{R}^2\} = (\infty, \infty)$ and $D_{out}^{-}V(\theta, D) = \{(p,q) \in \mathbb{R}^2 : \liminf \emptyset\} = (-\infty, -\infty)$. We know that for all $(p,q) \in D_{out}^{+}V(\theta, D)$ we have $\rho V(\theta, A) \geq \sup_{r<\bar{r}}\{u(\theta) - (p\alpha + q\gamma)(r - \bar{r})\}$ and for all $(p,q) \in D_{out}^{-}\ V(\theta, D)$ we have $\rho V(\theta, A) \leq \sup_{r<\bar{r}}\{u(\theta) - (p\alpha + q\gamma)(r - \bar{r})\}$. The optimal control at the border, i.e. $A = D$, must satisfy the following viscosity formalization of the Bellman equation:

$$\begin{aligned}\rho V(\theta, A) \geq u(\theta) &- \sup_{r<\bar{r}}\{(p_{out}\alpha + q_{out}\gamma)(r - \bar{r})\} I(r < \bar{r}) \\ &- \sup_{r\geq\bar{r}}\{(p\alpha + q\gamma)(r - \bar{r})\} I(r \geq \bar{r}), \\ &\text{for } (p_{out}, q_{out}) \in D_{out}^{+}V(\theta, D) \text{ and } (p,q) \in D^{+}V(\theta, D),\end{aligned}$$

$$\begin{aligned}\rho V(\theta, A) \leq u(\theta) &- \sup_{r<\bar{r}}\{(p_{out}\alpha + q_{out}\gamma)(r - \bar{r})\} I(r < \bar{r}) \\ &- \sup_{r\geq\bar{r}}\{(p\alpha + q\gamma)(r - \bar{r})\} I(r \geq \bar{r}), \\ &\text{for } (p_{out}, q_{out}) \in D_{out}^{-}V(\theta, D) \text{ and } (p,q) \in D^{-}V(\theta, D),\end{aligned}$$

where $I(.)$ is the indicator function. The only control r that fulfills both conditions is $r(t) \equiv \bar{r}$. Any $r(t) < \bar{r}$ would violate at least one condition. Thus, the optimal behavior is to conduct expansion policy, $r(t) = 0$, to maximize θ and immediately defend, $r(t) = \bar{r}$, when the regime is at stake.

This solution is a viscosity solution, i.e. the natural extension of the solution concept for the Bellman equation (6). It is well known that value functions in general are not continuously differentiable for some feasible states[10] and thus for these points the classical solutions do not apply. Viscosity solutions do apply also in many cases, where the value function is not continuously differentiable but necessarily coincides with the standard solution otherwise. Therefore, we could have restricted our analysis to the approach used for the border case $A = D$. However, for reasons of clarity and intuition, we first showed the classical approach and then the viscosity approach.

The viscosity solution implies that the optimal policy is to maximize the instantaneous utility and to not care about its fragility, i.e. rising stress. The fragility is recognized but not accounted for in the decision about the optimal interest rate until the immediate danger of a crisis emerges. Since an opt-out induces costs, the decision maker raises the interest rate to fend off the attack. Thereby, it is only necessary that costs exist no

[10] In fact, the value function is differentiable only at regular points.

matter how big they are. Thus, it could also be private costs, which would arise with a breakdown of the regime, that prompt the decision maker to raise the interest rates. In the next section we discuss a linear model of the original differential equations (3) and (4).

3.2. Extended Linear Version

3.2.1. Differential Equations and Time Paths

Now, we consider the case where $f_2(.)$, $g_2(.)$, and $g_3(.)$ are also linear functions. We will continue to use the coefficients α and γ and define $\frac{\partial f_2(.)}{\partial \theta(t)} = \beta$, $\frac{\partial g_2(.)}{\partial \theta(t)} = \delta$, and $\frac{\partial g_3(.)}{\partial A(t)} = \varepsilon$. The difference to the simple model is that the attack not only increases due to a low interest rate but also due to herding (ε) and bad fundamentals (δ). This creates a far richer set of policy options, trade-offs, and realistic settings. E.g. expansion policy, $r(t) = 0$, not necessarily leads to an attack. It might be possible that the herding effect and the interest rate effect are outweighed through the effect of good fundamentals, implying that speculators refrain from attacking, $\dot{A} \leq 0$.

The state vector now evolves according to:

$$\begin{pmatrix} \dot{\theta} \\ \dot{A} \end{pmatrix} = \begin{pmatrix} -\alpha(r(t) - \bar{r}) - \beta(\theta(t) - \bar{\theta}) \\ -\gamma(r(t) - \bar{r}) - \delta(\theta(t) - \bar{\theta}) + \varepsilon A(t) \end{pmatrix}. \tag{17}$$

Analogously to (6), the Bellman equation is given by

$$\begin{aligned} \rho V(\theta, A) &= \sup_r \left\{ u(\theta) + \frac{dV(\theta, A)}{dt} \right\} \\ &= \sup_r \{ u(\theta) - (V_\theta \alpha + V_A \gamma)(r - \bar{r}) \\ &\quad - V_\theta \beta \theta(t) - V_A(\delta\theta(t) - \varepsilon A(t)) \}. \end{aligned} \tag{18}$$

Since the Bellman equation (18) is again linear in the control variable, a bang-bang solution is optimal. This solution describes immediate shifts in the policy, i.e. jumps from one endpoint to the other in the control interval. To assure that the control is bounded (cf. chapter 3, Feichtinger and Hartl 1986), we restrict the interest rate to:

$$0 \leq r(t) \leq R. \tag{19}$$

Hence, the central bank policy switches between expansion, $r(t) = 0$, and defense, $r(t) = R$.

In addition we restrict the attack to be nonnegative and less or equal the amount of reserves, i.e.

$$0 \leq A \leq D. \tag{20}$$

Solving the differential equations (17) gives the paths of the fundamentals for expansion policy $\theta(t)_{r=0}$ and for defense policy $\theta(t)_{r=R}$:[11]

$$\theta(t)_{r=0} = \theta_S \exp(-\beta t) + \theta_{\dot{\theta}=0,0}(1 - \exp(-\beta t)), \tag{21}$$

$$\theta(t)_{r=R} = \theta_S \exp(-\beta t) + \theta_{\dot{\theta}=0,R}(1 - \exp(-\beta t)). \tag{22}$$

The fundamentals process is driven by the policy decision and the mean reversion. Without policy intervention, i.e. the interest rate equals its natural rate, fundamentals converge to their natural level $\bar{\theta}$.

If the interest rate is set to $r(t) = 0$, an expansionary effect on the fundamentals is induced, that allows to boost the steady state of the fundamentals above their natural level to: $\theta_{\dot{\theta}=0,0} = \bar{\theta} + \frac{\alpha}{\beta}\bar{r}$. For defense policy, i.e. $r(t) = R$, the fundamentals steady state is lower than the natural level: $\theta_{\dot{\theta}=0,R} = \bar{\theta} + \frac{\alpha}{\beta}(\bar{r} - R)$, since $R > \bar{r}$.[12]

The paths (21) and (22) describe the evolution of θ in time t for an arbitrary starting point θ_S. If $t = 0$, then $\theta(0) = \theta_S$. When time passes the value of $\theta(t)$ moves from its starting point θ_S to its steady state $\theta_{\dot{\theta}=0,i}$ under the respective policy i.

Accordingly the paths of the attack for expansion policy $A(t)_{r=0}$ and for defense policy $A(t)_{r=R}$ are given by:[13]

$$\begin{aligned} A(t)_{r=0} = {} & A_S \exp(\varepsilon t) + \frac{1}{\varepsilon}\left(\frac{\alpha\delta}{\beta} - \gamma\right)\bar{r}(1 - \exp(\varepsilon t)) \\ & + \frac{\delta}{\varepsilon + \beta}\left(\theta_S - \theta_{\dot{\theta}=0,0}\right)(\exp(-\beta t) - \exp(\varepsilon t)), \end{aligned} \tag{23}$$

$$\begin{aligned} A(t)_{r=R} = {} & A_S \exp(\varepsilon t) + \frac{1}{\varepsilon}\left(\frac{\alpha\delta}{\beta} - \gamma\right)(\bar{r} - R)(1 - \exp(\varepsilon t)) \\ & + \frac{\delta}{\varepsilon + \beta}\left(\theta_S - \theta_{\dot{\theta}=0,R}\right)(\exp(-\beta t) - \exp(\varepsilon t)). \end{aligned} \tag{24}$$

The first term shows the herding effect of the attack. For positive initial values A_S,

[11] Derivations of all time paths are given in appendix 5.3.1.

[12] To clarify the notation we introduce labels for several important fundamental states. The indices show whether the motion in a state variable is zero, the policy chosen, and, if necessary, the state of the attack. E.g. the label $\theta_{\dot{\theta}=0,R}$ gives the location, where the motion of the fundamentals stops ($\dot{\theta} = 0$) for defense policy ($r = R$). An overview of the labels is given in appendix 5.1 on page 43.

[13] Obviously, the paths are only valid as long as the state restriction $0 \leq A \leq D$ admits to maintain a respective interest rate policy.

this effect increases the attack over time. The second term describes the interest rate elasticity of the attack. Reducing the interest rate is equal to reducing the financing costs of speculators, which increases the attack. For defense policy $R > \bar{r}$ the costs of speculation are high and the second term decreases the attack level. The third term links the attack to the fundamental state. For good fundamentals, i.e. $\theta_S > \bar{\theta} + \frac{\alpha}{\beta}\bar{r}$, a successful attack is unlikely. The good fundamentals lead to a reduced expected payoff and the attack decreases over time. For states worse than the respective steady state the expected payoff is high and the attack increases.

An overview of the used variables describing the different fundamental states is given in appendix 5.1.

3.2.2. Model Dynamics

For a better understanding, we briefly summarize the policy options of the central bank that will be discussed in greater detail afterwards. The bang-bang solution only allows expansion or defense policy. Expansion policy boosts the fundamentals but also increases stress. At some time the attack will exhaust the reserves ($A = D$) and the central bank remains with three options: it can opt out, stop the attack ($\dot{A} = 0$), or conduct defense policy to completely fend off the attack ($\dot{A} < 0$). Option one requires no action, the regime would simply collapse. When choosing option two, the central bank has to choose the interest rate that stops the motion of the attack. Option three is to set the maximum interest rate, which allows to fend of the attack completely over time.[14] Necessarily, at some time the attack will cease ($A = 0$), giving the central bank the option to start again with expansion policy or to preserve the no stress state.

Figure I.13 on page 54 in the appendix shows vector fields of expansion and defense policy with sample trajectories of the central bank's options.

These options of the central bank and the resulting dynamics of the system are now discussed in detail. Thereby, we follow the order just presented and start with expansion policy, i.e. $r(t) = 0$. For a first orientation we draw a phase diagram in the state space (θ, A) (cf. figure I.1).

The θ, A space is crossed by zero motion lines (ZMLs), on which a differential equation equals zero, i.e. the motion in the respective state stops, i.e. $\dot{\theta} = \dot{A} = 0$.[15]

Proposition 2 *The expansion policy ZMLs do not intersect in the feasible attack state $0 < A < D$, whereas the attack ZML is to the right of the fundamental ZML $\theta_{\dot{\theta}=0,0} \leq \theta_{\dot{A}=0,0}$.*

[14]Due to the restrictions on the control not every option is possible in every state (cf. proposition 3).
[15]Derivations of the ZMLs are given in section 5.3.2 of the appendix.

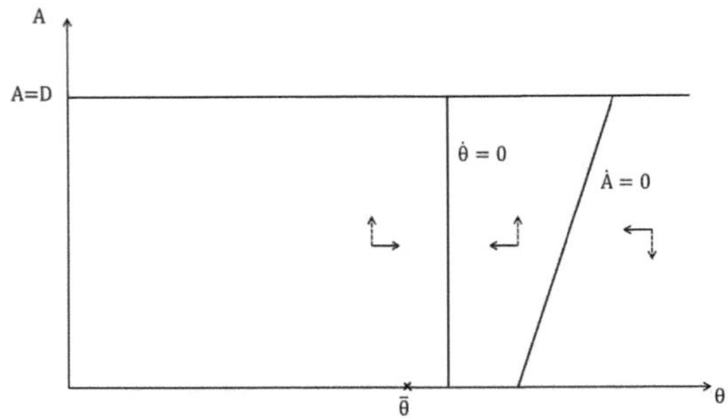

Figure I.1.: **Dynamics of expansion policy:** The arrows indicate the direction of the movement of the attack (dashed) and the fundamentals (solid). Fundamentals are drawn to their ZML ($\dot{\theta} = 0$), while the attack is pushed away of its ZML ($\dot{A} = 0$).

Solving the differential equations (17) for $r(t) = 0$ according to some initial value $\theta(0) = \theta_S$ respectively and equating, gives a negative attack level.[16]

The vertical line in figure (I.1) is the ZML of the fundamentals, $0 = \alpha\bar{r} - \beta\left(\theta(t) - \bar{\theta}\right)$, which is independent of the attack state. The diagonal line is the ZML of the attack, $0 = \gamma\bar{r} - \delta\left(\theta(t) - \bar{\theta}\right) + \varepsilon A(t)$. It states, that to offset a change in the attack at a higher attack level the fundamentals have to increase. Through the herding effect more speculators attack when the overall attack level increases. For a given interest rate, only a reduction in the expected payoff, i.e. higher fundamentals, can offset the motion in the attack, causing the positive slope of the attack ZML.

If the central bank sets the natural interest rate, $r(t) = \bar{r}$, the mean reversion pushes the fundamentals to their natural level $\bar{\theta}$. When choosing expansion policy, $r(t) = 0$, an economic growth effect of $\frac{\alpha}{\beta}\bar{r}$ is realized in addition to the natural level. Thus, the steady state for expansion policy equals $\bar{\theta} + \frac{\alpha}{\beta}\bar{r}$, which is also the location of the fundamental ZML. Fundamental states worse than this steady state exhibit a positive mean reversion, where better states exhibit a negative mean reversion. To the right of the attack ZML, the good fundamentals reduce the expected payoff of attacking so much, that, even if an attack is free of cost ($r(t) = 0$), stress declines. Thus, the fundamentals converge to their ZML whereas the attack diverges from its ZML. Depending on the starting point it is possible that a state trajectory crosses the attack ZML from right to left (cf. figure I.13).

Left to the attack ZML, expansion policy leads to increasing stress. Hence, after some time the attack will exhaust the reserves of the central bank. This attack state, where $A(t) = D$, we term high stress. In this case, the central bank's options—expansion and defense policy—widen by the possibility to stop the attack without fending it off

[16]Detailed proofs of propositions (2) - (5) are given in section 5.3.2 of the appendix.

completely. Therefore, the central bank chooses the smallest interest rate that offsets the motion of the attack, i.e. $r = \min\left\{r : \dot{A} = 0\right\}$. This stops the attack immediately, but causes an adaption of the fundamentals. To obtain a time path of the fundamentals during high stress, we solve the differential equations (17) for $\theta(t)$ with the additional restriction $\dot{A} = 0$ and get:[17]

$$\theta(t)_{A=D} = \theta_S \exp\left(\left(\frac{\alpha\delta}{\gamma} - \beta\right)t\right) + \widehat{\theta}_{A=D}\left(1 - \exp\left(\left(\frac{\alpha\delta}{\gamma} - \beta\right)t\right)\right). \tag{25}$$

Where θ_S is the fundamental value, in which the attack exhausts the reserves. If $\frac{\alpha\delta}{\gamma} - \beta > 0$, the fundamentals would converge to $\pm\infty$, depending on the initial position of θ_S. For fundamental states better than $\widehat{\theta}_{A=D}$, fundamentals would infinitely grow. For states worse, fundamentals would infinitely decline. Therefore, we imply the following condition on the parameters:

$$\frac{\alpha\delta}{\gamma} - \beta < 0. \tag{26}$$

Proposition 3 *Defense in high stress leads to a convergence point* $\left(\widehat{\theta}_{A=D}, D\right)$*, with* $\widehat{\theta}_{A=D} = \bar{\theta} + \frac{\frac{\alpha\varepsilon}{\gamma}D}{\frac{\alpha\delta}{\gamma} - \beta}$*. For* $R > \bar{r} - \frac{\varepsilon D}{\left(\frac{\alpha\delta}{\beta} - \gamma\right)}$ *(cf. 45) the point is accessible. Its fundamental state* $\widehat{\theta}_{A=D} \in \left[\theta^{A=D}_{\dot{A}=0,R}; \bar{\theta}\right[$*, i.e. its location, is between the attack ZML of defense policy and the no stress steady state.*

Defense in high stress stops the attack and leads to a convergence of the fundamentals. This is achieved by setting the interest rate to $r(t) = \bar{r} - \frac{\delta}{\gamma}\left(\theta_S - \bar{\theta}\right) + \frac{\varepsilon}{\gamma}D$, which is given by the differential equation of the attack (17). Note, that the interest rate has to rise when the fundamentals deteriorate. Bad fundamentals increase the chance of a successful attack and hence raise the expected payoff, which induces more speculators to attack. This can only be offset, if the central bank raises the costs of speculation through raising the interest rate. The worse the fundamentals, the higher the interest rate has to be to fend off additional speculators. The control restriction (19) on the interest rate implies a fundamental state θ, where $R = \max\left\{r : \dot{A} = 0\right\}$. This fundamental state coincides with the attack ZML of defense policy at $A = D$, which precisely defines the point where the growth of the attack stops. In every state worse, defense would require interest rates higher than R. Thus, defense is not possible and the central bank is forced to abandon the regime. On the other hand, better fundamental states reduce the expected payoff of an attack and thus induce more speculators to refrain from attacking. Hence, the control restriction implies another fundamental state θ, where $0 = \min\left\{r : \dot{A} = 0\right\}$. This

[17] The derivation is given in appendix 5.3.1.

fundamental state coincides with the attack ZML of expansion policy. For better states the attack decreases without an intervention of the central bank. Therefore, the path of the fundamentals in high stress is only valid in the interval $[\theta^{A=D}_{\dot{A}=0,R}, \theta^{A=D}_{\dot{A}=0,0}]$, i.e. between the attack ZMLs. Figure (I.2) shows the evolution of the interest rate (gray line) depending on the underlying fundamental state.

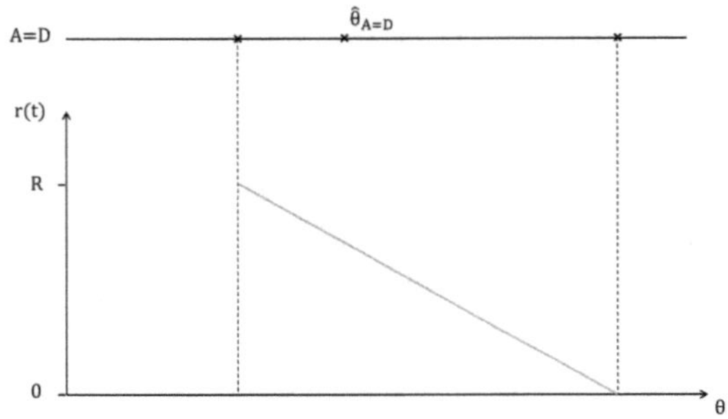

Figure I.2.: **Convergence in high stress:** The figure shows the evolution of the interest rate (gray line) depending on the fundamental state. Deteriorating fundamentals induce more speculators to attack and require higher interest rates to stop the attack. Convergence in high stress $A = D$ is only possible between the attack ZMLs $[\theta^{A=D}_{\dot{A}=0,R}, \theta^{A=D}_{\dot{A}=0,0}]$. See also figure I.3.

Proposition 4 *The defense policy ZMLs do not intersect in the feasible attack state* $0 < A < D$*, whereas the attack ZML is to the left of the fundamental ZML* $\theta_{\dot{A}=0,R} \leq \theta_{\dot{\theta}=0,R}$.

Solving the differential equations (17) for $r(t) = R$ according to $\theta(0) = \theta_S$, leads to an attack level higher than the stock of reserves.

When the central bank decides to defend, i.e. $r(t) = R$, the ZMLs shift and the dynamics change. The high interest rate increases the cost of credit and dampens the fundamentals by the amount $\frac{\alpha}{\beta}R$, compared to expansion policy. Hence, the steady state for defense policy is $\bar{\theta} + \frac{\alpha}{\beta}(\bar{r} - R)$, which equals the location of the ZML of the fundamentals. The high interest rate increases the costs for speculators and thereby reduces stress by $\frac{\gamma}{\delta}R$. Figure I.3 shows the phase diagram from above extended by defense policy.

Again fundamentals converge to their ZML, whereas the attack diverges from its ZML. Depending on the starting point it is possible that a state trajectory crosses the attack ZML from left to right.[18]

Defense policy leads to decreasing stress, so that the attack ceases after some time and the no stress region is reached: $A(t) = 0$. At this lower boundary the central bank has the choice to start again with expansion policy or to preserve the no stress state ($\dot{A} = 0$).

[18]A vector field with sample trajectories is given in appendix 5.3.2.

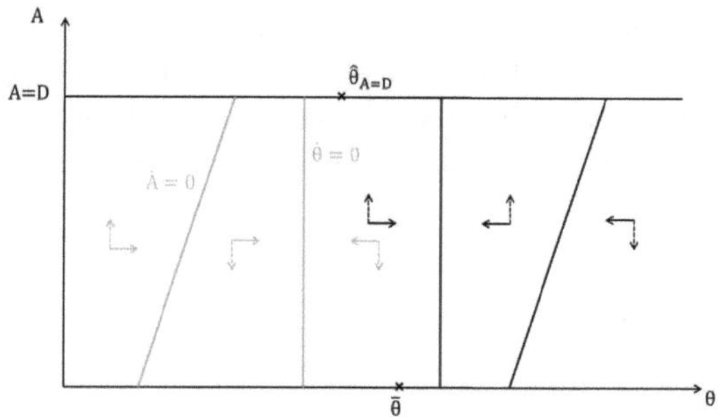

Figure I.3.: **Dynamics of expansion and defense policy:** The gray arrows indicate the direction of the movement of the attack (dashed) and the fundamentals (solid) under defense policy. Again fundamentals are drawn to their ZML ($\dot{\theta} = 0$), while the attack is pushed away of its ZML ($\dot{A} = 0$).

With deteriorating fundamentals the expected payoff of attacking rises, inducing more speculators to attack. To preserve the no stress state, the central bank has to raise the interest rate appropriately (cf. figure I.4). This increases the costs of speculation and induces more speculators to refrain from the attack. For fundamentals worse than the attack ZML of defense policy interest rates higher than the upper limit, R, would be required to successfully keep the no stress state. In this region the attack increases independent of the central bank policy.[19] For fundamentals better than the attack ZML of expansion policy, expected payoffs decrease so much, that even for an interest rate of zero the attack declines. Since the attack is restricted to nonnegative values it is assumed to equal zero in this region. Therefore, the time path of the fundamentals in no stress is

$$\theta\left(t\right)_{A=0} = \theta_S \exp\left(\left(\frac{\alpha\delta}{\gamma} - \beta\right)t\right) + \widehat{\theta}_{A=0}\left(1 - \exp\left(\left(\frac{\alpha\delta}{\gamma} - \beta\right)t\right)\right). \tag{27}$$

The path is valid for $\theta_S \geq \bar{\theta} + \frac{\gamma}{\delta}\left(\bar{r} - R\right)$. Note that this implies that the path is valid beyond the attack ZML of expansion policy in no stress. The gray line in figure I.4 shows the evolution of the interest rate in no stress.

Proposition 5 *The convergence point in no stress* $\left(\widehat{\theta}_{A=0}, 0\right)$ *equals the natural rate of the fundamentals* $\bar{\theta} \in \left]\widehat{\theta}_{A=D}; \theta_{\dot{\theta}=0,0}\right[$, *i.e. its location is between the convergence point in high stress and the fundamental ZML of expansion policy.*

Due to the herding effect more speculators attack for a given fundamental state with increasing stress. To stop the attack the interest rate has to increase according to the

[19] Obviously, the speed of change is still influenced through the policy decision.

level of stress. Consequently, the fundamentals in high stress are affected more than in no stress and converge to a lower fundamental state. Thus, the convergence point in no stress is in a better fundamental state than the convergence point in high stress $\widehat{\theta}_{A=0} > \widehat{\theta}_{A=D}$. Therefore, we term $\widehat{\theta}_{A=0}$ good focal point and $\widehat{\theta}_{A=D}$ bad focal point.

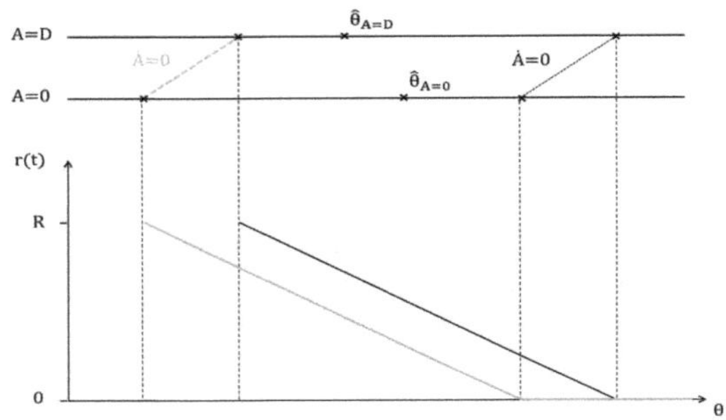

Figure I.4.: **Convergence in no stress:** Deteriorating fundamentals require higher interest rates to stop speculators from attacking. Convergence in no stress $A = 0$ is possible to the right of the attack ZML of defense policy, $[\theta^{A=0}_{\dot{A}=0,R}, \infty[$. The gray line shows the interest rate that is necessary to stop the attack in no stress.

3.2.3. Optimal Behavior

Numerical Example Due to the imposed control restriction, state restriction, and terminal condition we could not obtain a closed solution of the Bellman and the Hamiltonian approach. Therefore, we present numerical solutions of optimal policies in specified areas of the state space. The following parameters resemble a heuristic calibration of a developed country:

$$\alpha = 0.1, \beta = 0.2, \gamma = 0.2, \delta = 0.3, \varepsilon = 0.05, R = 12, \bar{r} = 3, \bar{\theta} = 2, D = 8.$$

Starting in the no stress steady state $(\theta_S, A_S) = (\bar{\theta}, 0)$ the periodic natural growth rate $\bar{\theta}$ is equal to 2%, the according natural interest rate $\bar{r}$ is 3%. If the central bank conducts expansion policy, $r(t) = 0$, this improves fundamentals' growth by $-\alpha(0 - \bar{r}) = 0.3\%$ inducing a mean reversion effect of $-\beta(2.3 - \bar{\theta}) = -0.06\%$. Note that this example should only give an intuition about the impact of the effects and does not represent the continuous effects exactly. In the long run, expansion policy can improve the growth rate from 2% to $\bar{\theta} + \frac{\alpha}{\beta}\bar{r} = 3.5\%$. However, expansion policy allows to speculate at zero costs. Hence, the motion of the attack, initially at zero, increases by $-\gamma(0 - \bar{r}) = 0.6\%$. The increase is amplified through the herding effect: $\varepsilon \cdot 0.6 = 0.03\%$. However, both effects are offset through the improving fundamentals and the accompanied decrease in the expected payoff to attacking. This reduces the growth of the attack by: $-\delta\left(2.3-\bar{\theta}\right) = -0.09\%$. In this example the initial point was in the no stress steady state. Expansion policy increased the fundamentals at the cost of increased stress. Here, it would take 16.7 periods until the ongoing attack exhausts the reserves. In initial states worse, the terminal time is significantly smaller, e.g. for $\theta_S = -8$ it takes only 2.6 periods from an environment with initially no stress to reach high stress, with the regime being at stake.

Identity Line When comparing the value of expansion policy and defense policy a crucial question determining the overall outcome is: where is the locus[20] of the fundamental path and how long does it take, till one of the state constraints of the attack is reached? Since the terminal time T has no closed solution, we can only argue that e.g. the state at termination for expansion policy is smaller than for defense policy, $\theta_{T_{r=0}} < \theta_{T_{r=R}}$. This is the case if the slope of the trajectory in the state space $\left(\frac{\partial A}{\partial \theta}\right)$ is always higher under expansion policy than under defense policy. Therefore, we look for a curve on which the slopes of the trajectories of expansion and defense are equal. We call this curve identity line.

Proposition 6 *On an identity line the slope of the state space trajectory under expansion policy equals the slope of the state space trajectory under defense policy, i.e.* $\frac{\partial A_{r=0}}{\partial \theta_{r=0}} = \frac{\partial A_{r=R}}{\partial \theta_{r=R}}$. *Since the direction of the motion changes depending on the location, it is necessary to also compute:* $\frac{\partial A_{r=0}}{\partial \theta_{r=0}} = -\frac{\partial A_{r=R}}{\partial \theta_{r=R}}$. *Consequently, we get two equations that define the identity lines.*

$$A_S = \left(\theta_S - \bar{\theta}\right)\frac{\frac{\alpha\delta}{\gamma}-\beta}{\frac{\alpha\varepsilon}{\gamma}} \text{ and } A_S = -\frac{1}{\varepsilon}\left(\gamma\bar{r} - \delta\left(\theta_S-\bar{\theta}\right) + \frac{\gamma R\left(\alpha\bar{r}-\beta\left(\theta_S-\bar{\theta}\right)\right)}{\alpha R - 2\left(\alpha\bar{r}-\beta\left(\theta_S-\bar{\theta}\right)\right)}\right) \tag{28}$$

The focal points $\widehat{\theta}_{A=0}$ and $\widehat{\theta}_{A=D}$ lie on the identity line.[21]

The identity lines separate the θ, A space into four areas (cf. figure I.5). Since the motion of the fundamentals stops at the fundamental ZML, the slope of the trajectory rises infinitely. Hence, around the fundamental ZML of expansion policy, the slope of the trajectory under expansion is higher than under defense. Since the motion in the attack stops at the attack ZML, the slope of the trajectory converges to zero. Consequently, around the attack ZML of expansion policy, defense policy leads to a higher slope of the

[20]Locus refers to the location of a path in the state space.

[21]The proof and the derivation of the identity lines are in appendix 5.3.3.

trajectory. Figure I.5 shows the identity lines as well as the four areas and marks which policy alternative leads to a higher slope of a state space trajectory.[22]

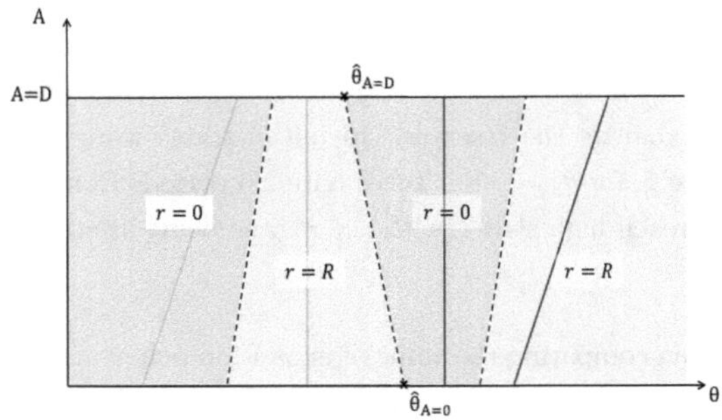

Figure I.5.: **Identity lines:** On the identity lines (dashed) the slope of the state space trajectories are equal for expansion and defense. The shaded areas show, whether the trajectory under expansion policy ($r = 0$) has a higher slope or the trajectory under defense policy ($r = R$).

Value of Convergence Points

Proposition 7 *For sufficiently high time preference the bad focal point $\widehat{\theta}_{A=D}$ is stable, while the good focal point $\widehat{\theta}_{A=0}$ is unstable. Choosing defense in the bad focal point leads to an immediate loss in the fundamentals, while choosing expansion in the good focal point increases the fundamentals further.*

Starting from the bad focal point $\widehat{\theta}_{A=D}$, the central bank can produce a closed loop (cf. figure I.6). Therefore, it defends for some time, then expands till the reserves are again exhausted[23] and finally stops the attack to converge back to the bad focal point. During defense the slope of the trajectory exceeds the slope during expansion. After passing the identity line, the slope under expansion exceeds the slope under defense. This track leads to a fundamental state at the time the reserves are exhausted again that is better than the bad focal point. For a sufficiently high time preference, the central bank will avoid current losses and will not deviate from the bad focal point. Panel (a) of figure I.7 shows the evolution of the instantaneous utility (gray line) for a one period deviation from the bad focal point (dashed gray line).

The central bank can also produce a closed loop starting from the good focal point $\widehat{\theta}_{A=0}$ (cf. figure I.6). Therefore, it expands for some time, then defends till the attack ceases

[22] A formal proof is given in appendix 5.3.3.

[23] When speculators refrain from attacking, they buy back the currency to settle their accounts, thereby restoring the reserves of the central bank.

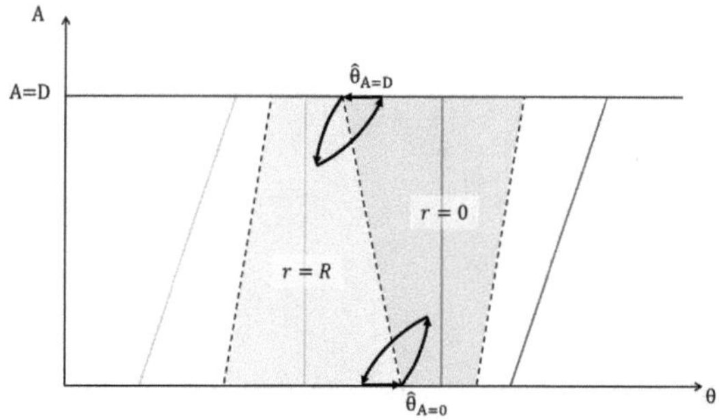

Figure I.6.: **Closed loops:** The figure shows the paths of short-term deviations from the focal points.

and converges back to the good focal point. During expansion the slope of the trajectory exceeds the slope during defense. After passing the identity line, the slope under defense exceeds the slope under expansion. Thus, the fundamental state in which no stress is reached is lower than the good focal point. Hence, a current profit in instantaneous utility can be exchanged with a future loss in instantaneous utility. A sufficiently high time preference induces the central bank to deviate from the good focal point. But, having a high time preference, the central bank has no reason to defend after some time, since defense would cause lower fundamentals than expansion. When the central bank sticks to the expansion policy, it will reach high stress after some time and consequently end up in the bad focal point, which is stable if time preference is high. However, having a low time preference, the central bank will bear the current loss, induced by a deviation from the bad focal point, and defend to reach the good focal point, which is stable for a low time preference. Panel (b) of figure I.7 shows the evolution of the instantaneous utilities for a transition from the good to the bad focal point, in case of high time preference, as well as the transition from the bad to the good focal point, in case of low time preference.

Comparison of Values In section 3.2.2 we showed that stopping the attack ($\dot{A} = 0$) in no stress is only possible to the right of the attack ZML of defense policy. In high stress the attack can only be stopped between the attack ZMLs. The options of the central bank depend on the fundamental state at the time when the attack meets the state restriction (20). Therefore, we define sets of starting points that lead to the same state restrictions. Thereby, we identify three areas (cf. figures I.8 and I.13). From area one all paths lead to a forced opt-out. From area three all paths lead to a temporary convergence in no

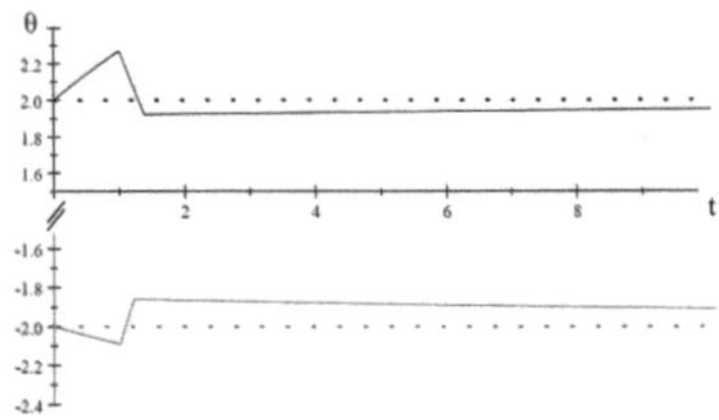

(a) short-term

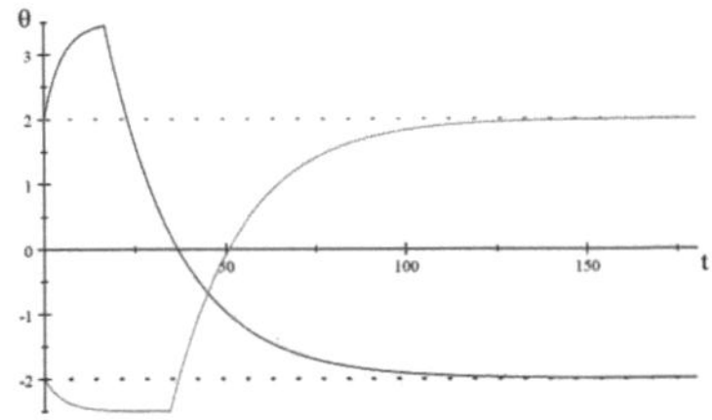

(b) long-term

Figure I.7.: **Focal points:** The panels show the evolution of the instantaneous utility for short-term deviations and long-term convergence from the good ($\widehat{\theta}_{A=0} = 2$) and bad ($\widehat{\theta}_{A=D} = -2$) focal points. The plots are based on the aforementioned parameter values.

stress.[24,25] Note that an evolution into area one and three is not possible if the starting point is outside these areas. In area two, defense leads to convergence in no stress, while expansion leads to high stress and the choice to converge or to opt out.[26]

In the remainder of the section, we compare the values of expansion and defense policy for starting points from the three areas.

Proposition 8 *Area 1: for a sufficiently high time preference, the value of expansion policy and opt-out is higher than the value of defense policy and opt-out:*

$$\int_0^{T_{r=0}} \exp(-\rho t)\left(\theta(t)_{r=0}\right) dt + \exp(-\rho T_r)\frac{1}{\rho}\left(\theta_{T_{r=0}} - c\right)$$
$$> \int_0^{T_{r=R}} \exp(-\rho t)\left(\theta(t)_{r=R}\right) dt + \exp(-\rho T_R)\frac{1}{\rho}\left(\theta_{T_{r=R}} - c\right). \quad (29)$$

Where $\theta(t)_{r=0}$ is the path of the fundamentals for expansion policy and $\theta(t)_{r=R}$ the path for defense policy. The starting point (θ_S, A_S) is in area one. The moment the level of the attack reaches the defensive measure is indicated by the terminal time T_i. Where $T_{r=0} = \inf\{t : A_{r=0}(t) > D\}$ and $T_{r=R} = \inf\{t : A_{r=R}(t) > D\}$. The corresponding value

[24] With expansion policy leading to the higher slope in area one, the state trajectory of defense policy with starting point $\left(\theta^{A=D}_{\dot{A}=0,R}, D\right)$ and time running in reverse gives the area of starting points that finally lead to an opt-out.
In area three we look for all paths that lead to a no stress state. Here, defense policy leads to the higher slope, implying that the state trajectory of expansion policy with starting point $\left(\theta^{A=0}_{\dot{A}=0,r}, 0\right)$ and time running in reverse gives the area of starting points leading to no stress.

[25] Obviously, convergence in no stress leads to area two, but for reasons of clarity, area three is analyzed separately.

[26] In section 5.3.2 of the appendix we plot vector fields of the differential system for expansion and defense policy (figure I.13 on page 54). As illustration, we highlighted some sample trajectories that show the evolution from starting points of the different areas. The trajectories are marked with the according area.

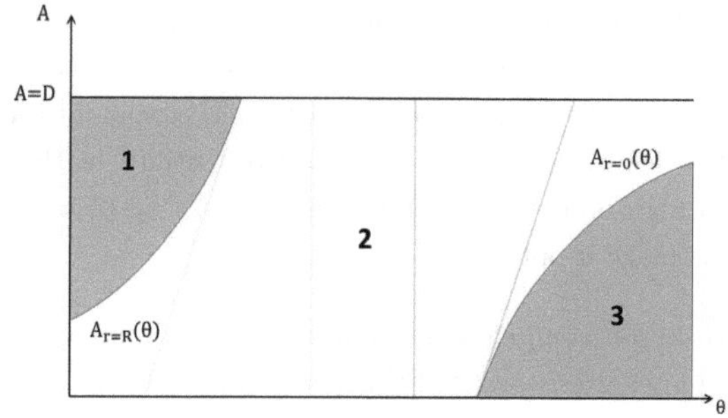

Figure I.8.: **Separation of paths:** The shaded areas contain the sets of initial values (θ_S, A_S) from which both policies lead to the same state restriction. For sample trajectories see also figure I.13.

of the fundamentals is θ_{T_i}. Expansion policy increases the fundamentals $\dot{\theta}_{r=0} > \dot{\theta}_{r=R} > 0$ but does not restrain the attack $\dot{A}_{r=0} > \dot{A}_{r=R} > 0$. However, the regime under expansion is terminated earlier: $T_{r=0} < T_{r=R}$. In area one the slope of the state trajectory is higher under expansion than under defense. Hence, the fundamental state in which reserves are exhausted is lower for expansion policy: $\theta_{T_{r=0}} < \theta_{T_{r=R}}$.

From the perspective of expansion policy, the trade-off is: there is a faster increase in fundamentals with early costs of opt-out, opposite to a slower, but higher, increase in fundamentals with postponed costs of opt-out. Figure I.9 shows a numerical sample plot of the instantaneous utilities of both policies with starting points in area one (defense policy is gray, expansion policy is black).[27]

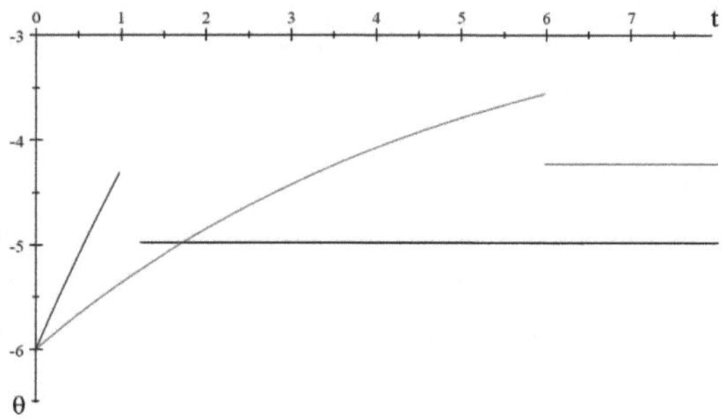

Figure I.9.: Instantaneous utility of expansion (black) and defense (gray) with inevitable opt-out.

The lower the initial attack level, the longer expansion policy can accumulate a higher utility compared to defense policy. However, the postponed regime switch allows defense

[27]Since utility is the identity function it is necessary that $\theta = u(\theta)$.

policy to achieve a higher instantaneous utility in the long run. What policy is better, is calculated by discounting the instantaneous utilities and adding them up to the current value of the respective path. Thus, the discount factor ρ is crucial for the overall outcome. Even if defense policy leads to a higher instantaneous utility in the long run, a high discount factor, i.e. a high preference for the present, can lead to a higher current value of expansion and thus make it optimal.

Proposition 9 *Area 2: for a sufficiently high time preference, the value of expansion policy and converging in high stress is higher than the value of defense policy and converging in no stress:*

$$\begin{aligned} &\int_0^{T_{r=0}^{A=D}} \exp(-\rho t)\left(\theta(t)_{r=0}\right) dt + \int_{T_{r=0}^{A=D}}^{\infty} \exp(-\rho t)\left(\theta(t)_{A=D}\right) dt \\ &> \int_0^{T_{r=R}^{A=0}} \exp(-\rho t)\left(\theta(t)_{r=R}\right) dt + \int_{T_{r=R}^{A=0}}^{\infty} \exp(-\rho t)\left(\theta(t)_{A=0}\right) dt \end{aligned} \tag{30}$$

Where $\theta(t)_{A=D}$ is the path of the fundamentals for convergence in high stress $A = D$ and $\theta(t)_{A=0}$ is the path of fundamentals for convergence in no stress $A = 0$. The starting point (θ_S, A_S) is in area two. The moment the level of the attack reaches no stress is indicated by time $T_{r=R}^{A=0} = \min\{t : A_R(t) = 0\}$.

For an arbitrary starting point (θ_S, A_S) the instantaneous utility through expansion policy grows faster in bad fundamental states and falls slower in good fundamental states, i.e. $\dot{\theta}_{r=0} > \dot{\theta}_{r=R}$. Defense policy reduces the level of stress in good states and slows down the increase in stress in bad states: $\dot{A}_{r=0} > \dot{A}_{r=R}$. Hence, expansion policy generates a higher instantaneous utility, but also admits higher stress that has to be dealt with. The bigger the attack in the initial starting point, the earlier expansion policy has to opt out or defend and there is less time to accumulate gains in instantaneous utility over defense policy.

The trade-off from the perspective of expansion policy is: initially higher fundamentals are followed by a long-term convergence to the bad focal point $\widehat{\theta}_{A=D}$ opposite to initially lower fundamentals with a long-term convergence to the good focal point $\widehat{\theta}_{A=0}$. However, for a sufficiently high time preference, the central bank values current more than future profits and losses, giving expansion policy a higher value than defense policy. Again a numerical example is plotted in figure I.10.

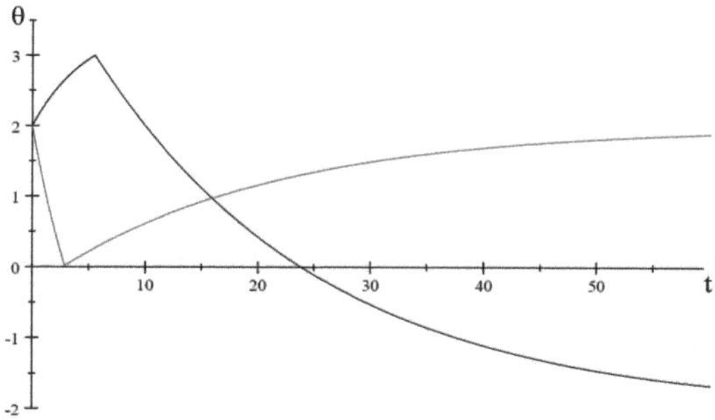

Figure I.10.: Instantaneous utility of expansion policy and convergence in high stress (black) versus defense policy and convergence in no stress (gray).

Proposition 10 *Area 2: for sufficiently high time preference, the value of expansion policy and opt-out is higher than the value of defense policy and converging in no stress:*

$$\int_0^{T_{r=0}} \exp(-\rho t)\left(\theta(t)_{r=0}\right) dt + \exp(-\rho T_{r=0}) \frac{1}{\rho}\left(\theta_{T_{r=0}} - c\right)$$
$$> \int_0^{T_{r=R}^{A=0}} \exp(-\rho t)\left(\theta(t)_{r=R}\right) dt + \int_{T_{r=R}^{A=0}}^{\infty} \exp(-\rho t)\left(\theta(t)_{A=0}\right) dt \tag{31}$$

The dynamics are unchanged compared to the previous example except for the immediate opt-out of the central bank, when the reserves are exhausted. The trade-off is: the more favorable evolution of the fundamentals through expansion is now followed by an instant drop in value imposed through the costs of the regime change opposite to a less favorable evolution of fundamentals and convergence to the good focal point. Despite the costs of opt-out, a regime switch can be optimal since it allows the proceeding of a regime being in a no stress steady state at $\theta(T_{r=0}) - c$. If $\theta(T_{r=0}) - c$ is smaller than $\widehat{\theta}_{A=0}$, defense policy reaches a higher instantaneous utility over time and again the outcome of the value comparison depends on the time preference. If, however, $\theta(T_{r=0}) - c$ is greater or equal $\widehat{\theta}_{A=0}$, expansion and opt-out is optimal independent of the time preference (cf. figure I.11).

But, why should the central bank bear the costs of a change immediately, when it could also converge in high stress?

Proposition 11 *In high stress to abandon the regime instantly is the optimal decision for fundamental states* $\theta > \widehat{\theta}_{A=D} + c\frac{\frac{\alpha\delta}{\gamma}-\beta-\rho}{\frac{\alpha\delta}{\gamma}-\beta}$.[28]

[28]The proof is given in appendix 5.3.3.

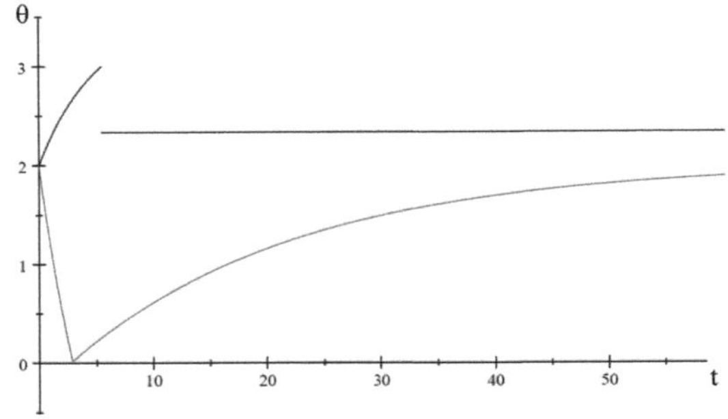

Figure I.11.: Instantaneous utility of expansion and opt-out (black) versus defense and convergence in no stress (gray).

When the reserves are exhausted in a very good fundamental state, it is better to abandon the regime immediately, bearing the costs, and prevent the fundamentals from further deterioration till the convergence point. The better the fundamentals the higher is the mean reversion effect and hence the loss through convergence. With higher costs of opt-out the immediate loss grows and therefore the fundamental state θ_c, above which an opt-out is optimal, increases too. Note that for high costs, i.e. $c > \frac{\bar{r}(\alpha\delta-\beta\gamma)-\beta\varepsilon D}{\delta\left(\frac{\alpha\delta}{\gamma}-\beta-\rho\right)}$, θ_c is to the right of the attack ZML of expansion policy and cannot be reached. If the time preference increases, the costs have a higher influence on the decision of the central bank. Hence, an opt-out must permit a higher fundamental state if the time preference increases.

Proposition 12 *Area 3: for good fundamentals, independent of the time preference, expansion policy and converging in no stress is better than defense policy and converging in no stress:*

$$\begin{aligned}&\int_0^{T_{r=0}^{A=0}} \exp\left(-\rho t\right)\left(\theta\left(t\right)_{r=0}\right) dt + \int_{T_{r=0}^{A=0}}^{\infty} \exp\left(-\rho t\right)\left(\theta\left(t\right)_{A=0}\right) dt \\ &> \int_0^{T_{r=R}^{A=0}} \exp\left(-\rho t\right)\left(\theta\left(t\right)_{r=R}\right) dt + \int_{T_{r=R}^{A=0}}^{\infty} \exp\left(-\rho t\right)\left(\theta\left(t\right)_{A=0}\right) dt \end{aligned} \tag{32}$$

For starting points in area three of figure I.8 we have $\dot{\theta}_{r=R} < \dot{\theta}_{r=0} < 0$. Again, expansion policy leads to more favorable fundamentals than defense, but defense has a major effect on the attack $\dot{A}_{r=R} < \dot{A}_{r=0} < 0$. Therefore, the attack ceases earlier under defense policy $T_{r=0}^{A=0} > T_{r=R}^{A=0}$. To keep the no stress state, it is sufficient to set the interest rate to zero (cf. proposition 5). Hence, both policy alternatives converge to the good focal point. Since expansion started with a zero interest rate the fundamental state during expansion is greater or equal than the fundamental state during defense, so that the realized value during expansion is greater. Consequently, expansion policy is optimal independent of the time preference. Figure I.12 shows a numerical example of both policy alternatives.

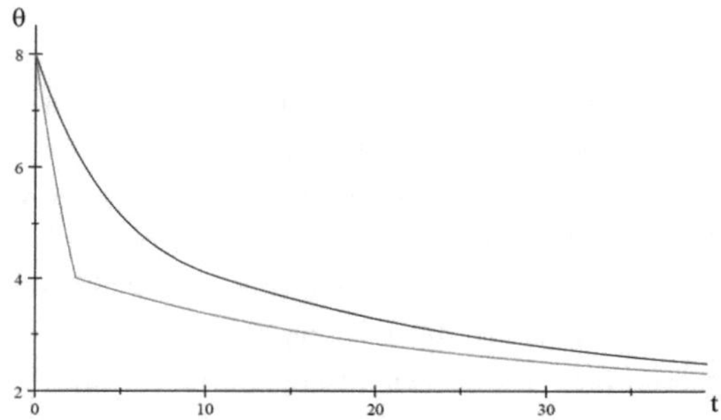

Figure I.12.: Instantaneous utility of defense and convergence in no stress (gray) versus expansion and convergence in no stress (black).

4. Conclusion

We applied an infinite horizon intertemporal optimization model with endogenous exit to a simple speculative attack framework. The central bank sets the interest rate which influences both fundamentals and attack strength. Hence, with one variable the central bank improves fundamentals but also increases stress. The central bank's role is beyond solely responding to speculative pressure or signaling. Depending on the current state the decision of the central bank has different implications for its own future position. Consequently, the central bank has to weigh the different outcomes against each other. If there is no dominant path, the optimal policy depends on the time preference of the central bank.

In the reduced linear model the interest rate is the only variable that influences and controls the state variables. Since there are no feedback effects, the motion in the attack can be stopped in no stress as well as in high stress without causing an adaption in the fundamentals. The central bank expands till the reserves are exhausted and the decision is between: stop the attack or allow a costly regime switch. Then the central bank raises the interest rate and remains in high stress.

We extend the model through allowing for fundamental feedback effects and a herding effect. In this extended linear model two focal points emerge. For a given policy and the necessary adaption at the state restriction the state trajectory ends up in one of the focal points.

The good focal point is characterized by a better fundamental state and lower interest rate. In high stress, through the herding effect, more speculators have to be fend off, which is done by raising the interest rate. However, the higher interest rate reduces the fundamentals which also induces higher speculative pressure that has to be fend off through an even higher interest rate.

Through a temporary deviation, expansion from the good focal point improves the fundamental state. With a subsequent defense and convergence back to the good focal point the central bank can produce a closed loop. In our numeric example the accumulated utility through the loop, after an expansion for 1 period, is for the first 3.7 periods higher than remaining at the good focal point. Thus, there is a huge incentive problem, if favorable short-term results give an advantage to the policy maker, who is subject to short mandates or reelections. Independency and low time preference, through long mandates and intermediate to long-term policy goals, are necessary to not put too much weight on the present. With a high time preference and the resulting high value of the present the central bank deviates from the good focal point. But, there is no reason to stop the expansion after a short time because further expansion further increases the fundamentals. With this reasoning going on, the reserves will be exhausted through an increasing attack. Then, the high time preference will only allow one decision: to fend off additional speculators, since this avoids both, the immediate costs an of an opt-out as well as the high costs of reducing the attack. Hence, the high time preference central bank will end up in the bad focal point.

From the bad focal point a deviation is only possible through defense. A closed loop is then produced if the central bank expands and finally converges back to the bad focal point. Hence, current costs have to be weighed against future profits. In our numerical example it takes only 1.5 periods till the cumulated utility turns positive compared to remaining in the bad focal point. For a sufficiently high time preference, the bad focal point is stable, since current losses are weighed more. However, a low time preference central bank will deviate to achieve a higher future utility and higher overall profits. But, this argument is also valid after a short defense, hence for sufficiently low time preference the central bank will defend till the attack ceases and converge to the good focal point to achieve the maximum utility in the long run.

For some initial values the state and control restrictions prevent the convergence to the focal points. Therefore, we categorized the state space into three areas that lead to different policy options at the state restrictions (cf. figure I.8).

All areas have in common that expansion policy leads to more favorable fundamental states compared to defense policy. This holds as long as the policy is not changed or a state restriction is met that requires an adaption. On the contrary, defense policy leads to lower attack levels compared to expansion policy.

In area one, which is characterized through bad fundamentals and medium to high stress, expansion as wells as defense, both, lead to further increasing stress and improving fundamentals. The trajectories reach high stress at fundamental states where defense is not possible and a regime switch is forced. Expansion gives the advantage of a currently superior fundamental state at the cost of a lower steady state after the opt-out. Consequently, defense policy will have the higher cumulated utility over time, but time preference determines which policy is valued more. A high time preference central bank values current profits more than future losses and thus chooses expansion. Since an opt-out is inevitable, the outcome is analogous to the first generation models and the 'hell' of the second generation models.[29] The main difference is, that, with the option to defend, the central bank can influence the terminal time as well as the terminal value.

In area two, better fundamentals allow defense policy to succeed in reducing stress.[30] This gives the central bank the opportunity to reach no stress and converge to the good focal point. Alternatively the central bank can conduct expansion policy and decide in high stress to either converge to the bad focal point or to opt out by choice. This regime switch induces a proceeding regime that—through conducting sound policy—persists in a steady state at a fundamental value of the terminal value minus the costs for the regime switch. Such an opt-out can only be optimal, if the costs of a regime switch are negligible and the time preference is not too high. Hence, an immediate opt-out is better than convergence to a lower fundamental state, if the costs and the time preference are low. For very good initial fundamental states the terminal value of the regime after costs might be better than the good focal point. In this case, expansion and opt-out is the dominant strategy independent of the time preference. This area can be compared to the 'purgatory' from the second generation and also to global games. While in second generation models the outcome—crisis or no crisis—depends on the expectations of investors, here, the time preference of the central bank sets the direction and yields a unique equilibrium. Moreover, loops as described in the global game literature are possible (cf. e.g. Angeletos et al. 2007). However, for a constant time preference the outcome is unique.

For higher costs, a high time preference central bank will avoid the detriments in fundamentals through defense. In fact, it will conduct expansion policy and converge in high stress. Conversely, a low time preference central bank will accept the preliminary lower fundamentals, through defense, to achieve a higher long run growth in the good focal point.

In area three, which is characterized through good fundamentals and medium to no stress, both policies lead to decreasing stress and deteriorating fundamentals. The trajectories reach no stress in an area where the attack can be stopped through a zero interest rate. Expansion profits from the good fundamental state that allows to continue expansion policy without having to bear increasing stress as in other states. When converging to the good focal point, the trajectories move into area two. Henceforward, the decision which policy is optimal is ambiguous and again depends on the time preference and the costs of an opt-out. Area three can be compared to the 'heaven' in the second generation models. Though, here area three is only a temporary stage before area two is reached and the central bank policy determines whether the economy evolves into the high stress region or stays in no stress.

[29]For a categorization of the states in the second generation see Jeanne (1999).

[30]Starting with bad fundamentals it takes some time till stress decreases under defense, since the trajectory must first cross the attack ZML of defense policy.

This temporary nature of 'heaven' and 'hell' explains why there is no empirical confirmation for these states. They only exist temporarily after big shocks.

In contrast to the second generation, where—ex post—the realization of the expectations is used to justify whether the regime is abandoned or not, here, the state of the economy justifies the outcome and the economy evolves according to the initial position and the policy chosen.

In summary, a high time preference central bank will end up in the bad focal point or, if bad fundamentals do not allow high stress defense and the opt-out is forced, a proceeding regime with lower steady state. Conversely, a low time preference central bank will end up in the good focal point or a proceeding regime with comparatively high steady state. For low costs of a regime change, not too high time preference, and good fundamentals an immediate opt-out is optimal compared to convergence in high stress as well as convergence in low stress. Therefore, the proceeding regime must have a steady state, i.e. terminal value minus costs, that is higher than the good focal point.

If one follows the principle that more is better, it is suggested that measures should be taken that reduce the time preference of the central bank. This assures that the central bank is willing to bear currently lower fundamentals to profit from a higher long-term growth, although naturally present consumption is preferred to future consumption. Hence, a central bank should be independent, have a long-term mandate, and pursue long-term goals like price stability.

Also this model is too rudimentary to provide a realistic setting of the emergence of currency crisis it offers useful insights in the various complications associated with policy choices and the paths that emerge.

Therefore, I apply our model to the Swedish currency crisis 1992. For a detailed description of the events during the Swedish crisis see Hörngren and Lindberg (1993). In 1991 the Riksbank decided to switch the peg from a trade weighted currency basket to a unilateral ECU peg. In September 1992 Sweden experienced a recession while its currency remained stable with overnight interest rates of 12%. However, on September 8th Finland abandoned its fixed exchange rate and simultaneously the confidence in the Swedish peg vanished with capital outflows increasing. To prevent this outflow the Riksbank raised the overnight interest rate to 75% which successfully fend off speculators. On September 15th speculation rose again, so that the central bank raised the overnight interest rate to 75% and to 500% the next day. After four days the situation relaxed and interest rates were lowered. However, in November pressure and—as a reply—interest rates rose again. Due to high costs the Riksbank decided to abandon the fixed exchange rate. In the context of our model Sweden was in area two to the right of the bad focal point. There, expansion policy improves fundamentals but also allows increasing stress. With the speculative attack increasing, defense becomes necessary, which results in decreasing fundamentals that become an increasing burden for the economy. Thereby, every expansion that is followed by a defense, in sum, reduces the fundamentals (area above the identity line). With the fundamentals decreasing, the required interest rate for a successful defense increases. The implied damaging effects for the economy—facing a convergence to the bad focal point—induced the Riksbank to finally opt-out.

For future research it would be useful to study different terminal regimes, not only a pressure free state. This would allow to analyze recurring attacks so that an initial avoidance of an attack is rewarded more. Including stress in the utility function might also give useful insights in that only the relative gain of fundamentals over stress is then pursued. Moreover, the linearity assumptions could be relaxed to allow for nonlinearities in the herding effect, the fundamental feedback effects, and the interest rate effects.

5. Appendix

5.1. List of Fundamental States

Label	Description	Expression
θ	fundamental state	
$\bar{\theta}$	natural growth rate of fundamentals, convergence point in no stress, no stress steady state	
$\theta_{\dot{\theta}=0,0}$	steady state for expansion policy, locus of the fundamental ZML	$\bar{\theta}+\frac{\alpha}{\beta}\bar{r}$
$\theta_{\dot{\theta}=0,R}$	steady state for defense policy, locus of the fundamental ZML	$\bar{\theta}+\frac{\alpha}{\beta}\left(\bar{r}-R\right)$
$\theta_{\dot{A}=0,0}$	locus of the attack ZML for expansion policy in no stress	$\bar{\theta}+\frac{\gamma}{\delta}\bar{r}$
$\theta^{A=D}_{\dot{A}=0,0}$	locus of the attack ZML for expansion policy in high stress	$\bar{\theta}+\frac{\gamma}{\delta}\bar{r}+\frac{\varepsilon}{\delta}D$
$\theta_{\dot{A}=0,R}$	locus of the attack ZML for defense policy in no stress	$\bar{\theta}+\frac{\gamma}{\delta}\left(\bar{r}-R\right)$
$\theta^{A=D}_{\dot{A}=0,R}$	locus of the attack ZML for defense policy in high stress	$\bar{\theta}+\frac{\gamma}{\delta}\left(\bar{r}-R\right)+\frac{\varepsilon}{\delta}D$
$\widehat{\theta}_{A=0}$	convergence point in no stress, natural growth rate	$\bar{\theta}$
$\widehat{\theta}_{A=D}$	convergence point in high stress	$\bar{\theta}+\frac{\frac{\alpha\varepsilon}{\gamma}D}{\frac{\alpha\delta}{\gamma}-\beta}$
θ_c	point of indifference between opt-out and convergence in high stress	$\widehat{\theta}_{A=D}+c\frac{\frac{\alpha\delta}{\gamma}-\beta-\rho}{\frac{\alpha\delta}{\gamma}-\beta}$

5.2. Linear Version

5.2.1. Value Function

Assuming exponential utility $u(\theta) = -exp(-\chi\theta)$, where χ is the risk aversion parameter we derive the value function for expansion policy and defense at $A = D$:

$$
\begin{aligned}
V &= \sup_r (U_0) \\
&= -\int_0^{T^{A=D}} \exp(-\rho t)\exp(-\chi(\theta + \alpha\bar{r}t))\,dt \\
&\qquad - \int_{T^{A=D}}^{\infty} \exp(-\rho t)\exp\left(-\chi\left(\theta + \alpha\bar{r}T^{A=D}\right)\right)dt \\
&= -\int_0^{T^{A=D}} \exp(-\rho t - \chi(\theta + a\bar{r}t))\,dt \\
&\qquad - \exp\left(-\chi\left(\theta + \alpha\bar{r}T^{A=D}\right)\right)\int_{T^{A=D}}^{\infty} \exp(-\rho t)\,dt \\
&= \left[\frac{\exp(-\rho t - \chi(\theta + \alpha\bar{r}t))}{\rho + \chi\alpha\bar{r}}\right]_0^{T^{A=D}} - \exp\left(-\chi\left(\theta + \alpha\bar{r}T^{A=D}\right)\right)\left[-\frac{\exp(-\rho t)}{\rho}\right]_{T^{A=D}}^{\infty} \\
&= \frac{\exp\left(-\rho T^{A=D} - \chi\left(\theta + \alpha\bar{r}T^{A=D}\right)\right)}{\rho + \chi\alpha\bar{r}} - \frac{\exp(-\chi\theta)}{\rho + \chi\alpha\bar{r}} \\
&\qquad - \frac{1}{\rho}\exp\left(-\rho T^{A=D} - \chi\left(\theta + \alpha\bar{r}T^{A=D}\right)\right) \\
&= \frac{\exp\left(-\rho T^{A=D} - \chi\left(\theta + \alpha\bar{r}T^{A=D}\right)\right)}{\rho + \chi\alpha\bar{r}} - \frac{\exp(-\chi\theta)}{\rho + \chi\alpha\bar{r}} \\
&\qquad - \frac{\exp\left(-\rho T^{A=D} - \chi\left(\theta + \alpha\bar{r}T^{A=D}\right)\right)\left(1 + \frac{1}{\rho}\chi\alpha\bar{r}\right)}{\rho\left(1 + \frac{1}{\rho}\chi\alpha\bar{r}\right)} \\
&= \frac{-\exp\left(-\rho T^{A=D} - \chi\left(\theta + \alpha\bar{r}T^{A=D}\right)\right)\frac{1}{\rho}\chi\alpha\bar{r} - \exp(-\chi\theta)}{\rho + \chi a\bar{r}} \\
&= -\frac{\exp(-\chi\theta)}{\rho + \chi\alpha\bar{r}}\left(\frac{\chi\alpha\bar{r}}{\rho}\exp\left(-(\rho + \chi\alpha\bar{r})T^{A=D}\right) + 1\right) < 0,
\end{aligned}
\tag{33}
$$

which is always negative.

The partial derivative of V with respect to θ is

$$
\begin{aligned}
&\frac{d}{d\theta}\left(-\frac{\exp(-\chi\theta)}{\rho + \chi\alpha\bar{r}}\left(\frac{\chi\alpha\bar{r}}{\rho}\exp\left(-(\rho + \chi\alpha\bar{r})T^{A=D}\right) + 1\right)\right) \\
&= -\chi V,
\end{aligned}
$$

which is always positive.

The partial derivative of V with respect to A is[31]

$$\begin{aligned}
&\frac{d}{dA}\left(-\frac{\exp\left(-\chi\theta\right)}{\rho+\chi\alpha\bar{r}}\left(\frac{\chi\alpha\bar{r}}{\rho}\exp\left(-\left(\rho+\chi\alpha\bar{r}\right)T^{A=D}\right)+1\right)\right)\\
&=-\frac{\exp\left(-\chi\theta\right)}{\rho+\chi\alpha\bar{r}}\left(\frac{\chi\alpha\bar{r}}{\rho}\exp\left(-T^{A=D}\left(\rho+\chi\alpha\bar{r}\right)\right)\right)\frac{\left(\rho+\chi\alpha\bar{r}\right)}{\gamma\bar{r}},
\end{aligned}$$

which is always negative. Using the expression for the value function (33), the partial derivative can also be written as

$$\begin{aligned}
&=\frac{\rho+\chi\alpha\bar{r}}{\gamma\bar{r}}\left(V+\frac{\exp\left(-\chi\theta\right)}{\rho+\chi\alpha\bar{r}}\right)\\
&=\frac{1}{\gamma\bar{r}}\Big(\left(\rho+\chi\alpha\bar{r}\right)V+\exp\left(-\chi\theta\right)\Big).
\end{aligned}$$

Using (7) we proof that an exterior solution exists. Therefore, it is necessary that:

$$\begin{aligned}
&V_\theta\alpha+V_A\gamma>0\\
&V_\theta\alpha+V_A\gamma=-\chi V\alpha+\frac{1}{\gamma\bar{r}}\Big(\left(\rho+\chi\alpha\bar{r}\right)V+\exp\left(-\chi\theta\right)\Big)\gamma\\
&\qquad=-\chi V\alpha+\frac{1}{\bar{r}}\rho V+\chi\alpha V+\frac{1}{\bar{r}}\exp\left(-\chi\theta\right)\\
&\qquad=\frac{1}{\bar{r}}\left(\rho V+\exp\left(-\chi\theta\right)\right),
\end{aligned}$$

for the proof, it is necessary that:

$$\rho V+\exp\left(-\chi\theta\right)>0.$$

Inserting for V gives

$$\begin{aligned}
\rho\left(-\frac{\exp\left(-\chi\theta\right)}{\rho+\chi\alpha\bar{r}}\left(\frac{\chi\alpha\bar{r}}{\rho}\exp\left(-\left(\rho+\chi\alpha\bar{r}\right)T^{A=D}\right)+1\right)\right)+\exp\left(-\chi\theta\right)&>0\\
-\frac{1}{\rho+\chi\alpha\bar{r}}\left(\chi\alpha\bar{r}\exp\left(-\left(\rho+\chi\alpha\bar{r}\right)T^{A=D}\right)+\rho\right)+1&>0\\
\frac{1}{\rho+\chi\alpha\bar{r}}\left(\chi\alpha\bar{r}\exp\left(-\left(\rho+\chi\alpha\bar{r}\right)T^{A=D}\right)+\rho\right)&<1\\
\chi\alpha\bar{r}\exp\left(-\left(\rho+\chi\alpha\bar{r}\right)T^{A=D}\right)+\rho&<\rho+\chi\alpha\bar{r}\\
\exp\left(-\left(\rho+\chi\alpha\bar{r}\right)T^{A=D}\right)&<1\\
-\left(\rho+\chi\alpha\bar{r}\right)T^{A=D}&<0,
\end{aligned}$$

[31]From (11) we know that $T^{A=D}=\frac{D-A_S}{\gamma\bar{r}}$ and therefore $\frac{dT^{A=D}}{dA}=-\frac{1}{\gamma\bar{r}}$.

which is true, since $T^{A=D} \geq 0$.

5.2.2. Comparison of Values

For $t > T^{A=D}$ the central bank sets $r = \bar{r}$, which implies that $\theta(t)$ is constant, i.e. $\dot{\theta} = 0$ and thus $\theta(t) = \theta_T$. For $v(\theta_T - c)$ we write:

$$\begin{aligned} V(\theta_T - c, A = D) &= \int_0^\infty \exp(-\rho\tau)\, v(\theta_T - c)\, dt \\ &= v(\theta_T - c)\frac{1}{\rho} \\ &= -\frac{1}{\rho}\exp(-\chi(\theta_T - c)). \end{aligned} \tag{34}$$

In comparison, V at point $A = D$ equals:

$$\begin{aligned} V(\theta_T, A = D) &= \int_0^\infty \exp(-\rho t)\, u(\theta)\, dt \\ &= u(\theta_T)\frac{1}{\rho} \\ &= -\frac{1}{\rho}\exp(-\chi\theta_T). \end{aligned} \tag{35}$$

If we compare equations (34) and (35), we see that indeed $V(\theta_T, A = D)$ is higher and thus, defending the regime at the corner is optimal.

5.3. Extended Linear Version

5.3.1. Differential Equations and Time Paths

Time Path of the Fundamentals The central bank sets the control $r(t)$ and chooses between expansion policy $r(t) = 0$ and defense policy $r(t) = R$ (cf. condition (19)). The differential equation of the fundamentals (17) for defense policy thus is:

$$\dot{\theta} = -\alpha(R - \bar{r}) - \beta\left(\theta(t) - \bar{\theta}\right). \tag{17}$$

Solving the differential equation for θ gives:

$$\beta\theta(t) + \frac{d\theta}{dt} = \alpha(\bar{r} - R) + \beta\bar{\theta}$$

$$\left(\beta\theta(t) + \frac{d\theta}{dt}\right)\exp(\beta t) = \left(\alpha(\bar{r} - R) + \beta\bar{\theta}\right)\exp(\beta t)$$

$$\frac{d}{dt}\left(\theta(t)\exp(\beta t)\right) = \left(\alpha(\bar{r} - R) + \beta\bar{\theta}\right)\exp(\beta t)$$

$$\int \frac{d}{dt}\left(\theta(t)\exp(\beta t)\right)dt = \int \left(\alpha(\bar{r} - R) + \beta\bar{\theta}\right)\exp(\beta t)\,dt$$

$$\theta(t)\exp(\beta t) = C_\theta + \frac{1}{\beta}\left(\alpha(\bar{r} - R) + \beta\bar{\theta}\right)\exp(\beta t)$$

$$\theta(t) = C_\theta\exp(-\beta t) + \bar{\theta} + \frac{\alpha}{\beta}(\bar{r} - R),$$

for $t = 0$

$$\theta_S - \bar{\theta} - \frac{\alpha}{\beta}(\bar{r} - R) = C_\theta$$

and thus

$$\theta(t) = \left(\theta_S - \bar{\theta} - \frac{\alpha}{\beta}(\bar{r} - R)\right)\exp(-\beta t) + \bar{\theta} + \frac{\alpha}{\beta}(\bar{r} - R)$$

which we write as

$$\boxed{\theta(t) = \theta_S\exp(-\beta t) + \left(\bar{\theta} + \tfrac{\alpha}{\beta}(\bar{r} - R)\right)(1 - \exp(-\beta t)).} \tag{22}$$

If the central bank conducts expansion policy, we get

$$\boxed{\theta(t) = \theta_S\exp(-\beta t) + \left(\bar{\theta} + \tfrac{\alpha}{\beta}\bar{r}\right)(1 - \exp(-\beta t)).} \tag{21}$$

Time Path of the Attack The differential equation of the attack is

$$\dot{A} = -\gamma(R - \bar{r}) - \delta\left(\theta(t) - \bar{\theta}\right) + \varepsilon A(t) \tag{17}$$

$$\dot{A} - \varepsilon A(t) = \gamma(\bar{r} - R) - \delta\theta(t) + \delta\bar{\theta}.$$

Inserting for $\theta(t)$ gives

$$\dot{A} - \varepsilon A(t) = \gamma(\bar{r} - R) - \delta\left(\theta_S - \bar{\theta} - \frac{\alpha}{\beta}(\bar{r} - R)\right)\exp(-\beta t) - \delta\bar{\theta} - \frac{\alpha\delta}{\beta}(\bar{r} - R) + \delta\bar{\theta}$$

$$\dot{A} - \varepsilon A(t) = -\delta\left(\theta_S - \bar{\theta} - \frac{\alpha}{\beta}(\bar{r} - R)\right)\exp(-\beta t) - \left(\frac{\alpha\delta}{\beta} - \gamma\right)(\bar{r} - R).$$

Solving for A gives:

$$\begin{aligned}
\int \frac{d}{dt} A(t) \exp(-\varepsilon t)\, dt &= -\int \delta \left(\theta_S - \bar{\theta} - \frac{\alpha}{\beta}(\bar{r} - R)\right) \exp((-\varepsilon - \beta)t)\, dt \\
&\quad - \int \left(\frac{\alpha\delta}{\beta} - \gamma\right)(\bar{r} - R) \exp(-\varepsilon t)\, dt \\
A(t) \exp(-\varepsilon t) &= \frac{\delta}{\varepsilon + \beta}\left(\theta_S - \bar{\theta} - \frac{\alpha}{\beta}(\bar{r} - R)\right) \exp((-\varepsilon - \beta)t) \\
&\quad + \frac{1}{\varepsilon}\left(\frac{\alpha\delta}{\beta} - \gamma\right)(\bar{r} - R)\exp(-\varepsilon t) + C_A \\
A(t) &= \frac{\delta}{\varepsilon + \beta}\left(\theta_S - \bar{\theta} - \frac{\alpha}{\beta}(\bar{r} - R)\right)\exp(-\beta t) + \frac{1}{\varepsilon}\left(\frac{\alpha\delta}{\beta} - \gamma\right)(\bar{r} - R) \\
&\quad + C_A \exp(\varepsilon t).
\end{aligned}$$

For $t = 0$

$$A_S - \frac{1}{\varepsilon}\left(\frac{\alpha\delta}{\beta} - \gamma\right)(\bar{r} - R) - \frac{\delta}{\varepsilon + \beta}\left(\theta_S - \bar{\theta} - \frac{\alpha}{\beta}(\bar{r} - R)\right) = C_A$$

and thus

$$\begin{aligned}
A(t) &= \frac{1}{\varepsilon}\left(\frac{\alpha\delta}{\beta} - \gamma\right)(\bar{r} - R) + \frac{\delta}{\varepsilon + \beta}\left(\theta_S - \bar{\theta} - \frac{\alpha}{\beta}(\bar{r} - R)\right)\exp(-\beta t) \\
&\quad + \left(A_S - \frac{1}{\varepsilon}\left(\frac{\alpha\delta}{\beta} - \gamma\right)(\bar{r} - R) - \frac{\delta}{\varepsilon + \beta}\left(\theta_S - \bar{\theta} - \frac{\alpha}{\beta}(\bar{r} - R)\right)\right)\exp(\varepsilon t).
\end{aligned}$$

The time path of the attack for defense policy is

$$\boxed{\begin{aligned} A(t) = A_S \exp(\varepsilon t) + \tfrac{1}{\varepsilon}\left(\tfrac{\alpha\delta}{\beta} - \gamma\right)(\bar{r} - R)(1 - \exp(\varepsilon t)) \\ + \tfrac{\delta}{\varepsilon + \beta}\left(\theta_S - \bar{\theta} - \tfrac{\alpha}{\beta}(\bar{r} - R)\right)(\exp(-\beta t) - \exp(\varepsilon t)), \end{aligned}} \tag{24}$$

for expansion policy we get

$$\boxed{\begin{aligned} A(t) = A_S \exp(\varepsilon t) + \tfrac{1}{\varepsilon}\left(\tfrac{\alpha\delta}{\beta} - \gamma\right)\bar{r}(1 - \exp(\varepsilon t)) \\ + \tfrac{\delta}{\varepsilon + \beta}\left(\theta_S - \bar{\theta} - \tfrac{\alpha}{\beta}\bar{r}\right)(\exp(-\beta t) - \exp(\varepsilon t)). \end{aligned}} \tag{23}$$

Time Path of the Fundamentals During High Stress Convergence At the upper boundary of the attack, $A = D$, the interest rate is chosen from the control interval $[0, R]$, to offset the motion of the attack, i.e. $\dot{A} = 0$. We apply these conditions to the differential equation of the attack (17) and get:

$$0 = -\gamma \left(r\left(t\right) - \bar{r}\right) - \delta\left(\theta\left(t\right) - \bar{\theta}\right) + \varepsilon D$$

Solving for the interest rate gives

$$r\left(t\right) = \bar{r} - \frac{\delta}{\gamma}\left(\theta\left(t\right) - \bar{\theta}\right) + \frac{\varepsilon}{\gamma}D. \tag{36}$$

Equation (36) shows that the interest rate $r\left(t\right)$ required to offset the attack increases when the fundamentals deteriorate and decreases when the fundamentals rise. Therefore, there are fundamental states where the attack cannot be offset since the required interest rate would exceed R. In this case, the central bank is forced to opt out. But there are also states in which the attack decreases, due to good fundamentals, even though the interest rate equals zero. The fundamental states corresponding to the control boundary are

$$\begin{aligned} r\left(t\right) = R &\leftrightarrow \theta = \bar{\theta} + \frac{\varepsilon}{\delta}D + \frac{\gamma}{\delta}\left(\bar{r} - R\right) \\ r\left(t\right) = 0 &\leftrightarrow \theta = \bar{\theta} + \frac{\varepsilon}{\delta}D + \frac{\gamma}{\delta}\bar{r}. \end{aligned} \tag{37}$$

Inserting $r\left(t\right)$ (eq. 36) in the differential equation of the fundamentals (17) gives

$$\begin{aligned} \dot{\theta} &= -\alpha\left(\left(\bar{r} - \frac{\delta}{\gamma}\left(\theta\left(t\right) - \bar{\theta}\right) + \frac{\varepsilon}{\gamma}D\right) - \bar{r}\right) - \beta\left(\theta\left(t\right) - \bar{\theta}\right) \\ &= \left(\frac{\alpha\delta}{\gamma} - \beta\right)\left(\theta\left(t\right) - \bar{\theta}\right) - \frac{\alpha\varepsilon}{\gamma}D. \end{aligned}$$

The path of the fundamentals at $A = D$ is thus

$$\frac{d\theta}{dt} - \left(\frac{\alpha\delta}{\gamma} - \beta\right)\theta\left(t\right) = -\left(\frac{\alpha\delta}{\gamma} - \beta\right)\bar{\theta} - \frac{\alpha\varepsilon}{\gamma}D$$

$$\begin{aligned} &\int \frac{d}{dt}\left(\theta\left(t\right)\exp\left(-\left(\frac{\alpha\delta}{\gamma} - \beta\right)t\right)\right)dt \\ &\quad = \int\left(-\left(\frac{\alpha\delta}{\gamma} - \beta\right)\bar{\theta} - \frac{\alpha\varepsilon}{\gamma}D\right) exp\left(-\left(\frac{\alpha\delta}{\gamma} - \beta\right)t\right)dt \end{aligned}$$

$$\theta(t)\exp\left(-\left(\frac{\alpha\delta}{\gamma}-\beta\right)t\right)$$
$$=C+\frac{1}{-\left(\frac{\alpha\delta}{\gamma}-\beta\right)}\left(-\left(\frac{\alpha\delta}{\gamma}-\beta\right)\bar{\theta}-\frac{\alpha\varepsilon}{\gamma}D\right)\exp\left(-\left(\frac{\alpha\delta}{\gamma}-\beta\right)t\right)$$

$$\theta(t)=C\exp\left(\left(\frac{\alpha\delta}{\gamma}-\beta\right)t\right)+\bar{\theta}+\frac{\frac{\alpha\varepsilon}{\gamma}D}{\frac{\alpha\delta}{\gamma}-\beta}.$$

For $t=0$

$$\theta_S-\bar{\theta}-\frac{\frac{\alpha\varepsilon}{\gamma}D}{\frac{\alpha\delta}{\gamma}-\beta}=C$$

and thus

$$\theta(t)=\left(\theta_S-\bar{\theta}-\frac{\frac{\alpha\varepsilon}{\gamma}D}{\frac{\alpha\delta}{\gamma}-\beta}\right)\exp\left(\left(\frac{\alpha\delta}{\gamma}-\beta\right)t\right)+\bar{\theta}+\frac{\frac{\alpha\varepsilon}{\gamma}D}{\frac{\alpha\delta}{\gamma}-\beta}.$$

Hence, the path of the fundamentals in high stress for $\theta\in\left[\bar{\theta}+\frac{\varepsilon}{\delta}D+\frac{\gamma}{\delta}(\bar{r}-R),\bar{\theta}+\frac{\varepsilon}{\delta}D+\frac{\gamma}{\delta}\bar{r}\right]$[32] is

$$\boxed{\theta(t)=\theta_S\exp\left(\left(\frac{\alpha\delta}{\gamma}-\beta\right)t\right)+\left(\widehat{\theta}_{A=D}\right)\left(1-\exp\left(\left(\frac{\alpha\delta}{\gamma}-\beta\right)t\right)\right).}\tag{25}$$

where $\widehat{\theta}_{A=D}=\bar{\theta}+\frac{\frac{\alpha\varepsilon}{\gamma}D}{\frac{\alpha\delta}{\gamma}-\beta}$ is the upper convergence point.

Time Path of the Fundamentals During No Stress Convergence At the lower boundary of the attack, $A=0$, the interest rate is chosen from the control interval $[0,R]$, to offset the motion of the attack, i.e. $\dot{A}=0$. Using these conditions with the differential equation of the attack (17) gives:

$$0=-\gamma(r(t)-\bar{r})-\delta\left(\theta(t)-\bar{\theta}\right)$$

and solving for the interest rate gives

$$r(t)=\bar{r}-\frac{\delta}{\gamma}\left(\theta(t)-\bar{\theta}\right).\tag{38}$$

As in high stress, the control restriction imposes a restriction on the fundamental state space in which the motion of the attack can be offset. For bad fundamentals, the attack grows even though the interest rate is set to R. The fundamental state corresponding to

[32]Defense in high stress is only possible between the attack ZMLs.

the control boundary is

$$r(t) = R \leftrightarrow \theta = \bar{\theta} + \frac{\gamma}{\delta}(\bar{r} - R). \tag{39}$$

Inserting $r(t)$ (eq. 38) in the differential equation of the fundamentals (17) gives

$$\begin{aligned}\dot{\theta} &= -\alpha\left(\left(\bar{r} - \frac{\delta}{\gamma}\left(\theta(t) - \bar{\theta}\right)\right) - \bar{r}\right) - \beta\left(\theta(t) - \bar{\theta}\right) \\ &= \left(\frac{\alpha\delta}{\gamma} - \beta\right)\left(\theta(t) - \bar{\theta}\right).\end{aligned}$$

The path of the fundamentals at $A = 0$, is

$$\frac{d\theta}{dt} - \left(\frac{\alpha\delta}{\gamma} - \beta\right)\theta(t) = -\left(\frac{\alpha\delta}{\gamma} - \beta\right)\bar{\theta}$$

$$\int \frac{d}{dt}\left(\theta(t)\exp\left(-\left(\frac{\alpha\delta}{\gamma} - \beta\right)t\right)\right)dt = -\int\left(\frac{\alpha\delta}{\gamma} - \beta\right)\bar{\theta}\exp\left(-\left(\frac{\alpha\delta}{\gamma} - \beta\right)t\right)dt$$

$$\theta(t) = C\exp\left(\left(\frac{\alpha\delta}{\gamma} - \beta\right)t\right) + \bar{\theta}.$$

For $t = 0$

$$\theta_S - \bar{\theta} = C$$

and thus

$$\theta(t) = \left(\theta_S - \bar{\theta}\right)\exp\left(\left(\frac{\alpha\delta}{\gamma} - \beta\right)t\right) + \bar{\theta}.$$

or

$$\theta(t) = \theta_S\exp\left(\left(\frac{\alpha\delta}{\gamma} - \beta\right)t\right) + \bar{\theta}\left(1 - \exp\left(\left(\frac{\alpha\delta}{\gamma} - \beta\right)t\right)\right).$$

For good states, there is an expected loss on attacking that actually allows to fend off additional speculators, even for negative interest rates. Since we restricted the interest rate to be nonnegative (19), we set $A = 0$ for states better than the attack ZML of expansion policy and neglect the theoretical negativity of A. The path of the fundamentals in no stress for $\theta \in \left[\bar{\theta} + \frac{\gamma}{\delta}(\bar{r} - R), \infty\right[$ is:

$$\boxed{\theta(t) = \theta_S\exp\left(\left(\tfrac{\alpha\delta}{\gamma} - \beta\right)t\right) + \widehat{\theta}_{A=0}\left(1 - \exp\left(\left(\tfrac{\alpha\delta}{\gamma} - \beta\right)t\right)\right),} \tag{27}$$

where $\widehat{\theta}_{A=0} = \bar{\theta}$.

5.3.2. Model Dynamics

Zero-Motion-Lines To describe the direction of the movement of the state variable we calculate zero-motion-lines (ZMLs). The differential equation of the fundamentals (17) for $r(t) = R$ is: $\dot{\theta}_{r=R} = -\alpha(R - \bar{r}) - \beta(\theta_{\dot{\theta}=0,R} - \bar{\theta})$. Equating with zero and solving for θ gives:

$$\theta_{\dot{\theta}=0,R} = \bar{\theta} - \frac{\alpha}{\beta}(R - \bar{r}) \tag{40}$$

accordingly for $r(t) = 0$

$$\theta_{\dot{\theta}=0,0} = \bar{\theta} + \frac{\alpha}{\beta}\bar{r} \tag{41}$$

Since the ZMLs of the fundamentals are independent of A they are vertical lines in the θ,A space.

Equating the differential equation of the attack (17) for $r(t) = R$ with zero $\dot{A} = -\gamma(R - \bar{r}) - \delta(\theta_{\dot{A}=0,R} - \bar{\theta}) + \varepsilon A = 0$ and solving for θ gives:

$$\theta_{\dot{A}=0,R} = \bar{\theta} - \frac{\gamma}{\delta}(R - \bar{r}) + \frac{\varepsilon}{\delta}A \tag{42}$$

accordingly for $r(t) = 0$

$$\theta_{\dot{A}=0,0} = \bar{\theta} + \frac{\gamma}{\delta}\bar{r} + \frac{\varepsilon}{\delta}A \tag{43}$$

The ZMLs of the attack have a positive slope of $\frac{\varepsilon}{\delta}$ in the θ,A space.

Proof of proposition 2: we proof by contradiction and show that the intersection of the expansion policy ZMLs (41) and (43) violates the state restriction (20). That is $\bar{\theta} + \frac{\alpha}{\beta}\bar{r} \neq \bar{\theta} + \frac{\gamma}{\delta}\bar{r} + \frac{\varepsilon}{\delta}A$, for $A \in [0, D]$. Reorganizing gives: $\frac{1}{\varepsilon}\left(\frac{\alpha\delta}{\beta} - \gamma\right)\bar{r} \neq A$. With restriction (26), $\frac{\alpha\delta}{\beta} - \gamma < 0$, we get: $A < 0$ for an intersection of the expansion policy ZMLs.

Since expansion policy ZMLs only intersect for a negative attack value and the attack ZML has a positive slope, the fundamental ZML lies on the left side of the attack ZML in the feasible state.

Proof of proposition 3: when the central bank stops the attack ($\dot{A} = 0$) in high stress ($A = D$) the evolution of fundamentals is given by

$$\theta(t)_{A=D} = \theta_S \exp\left(\left(\frac{\alpha\delta}{\gamma} - \beta\right)t\right) + \left(\bar{\theta} + \frac{\frac{\alpha\varepsilon}{\gamma}D}{\frac{\alpha\delta}{\gamma} - \beta}\right)\left(1 - \exp\left(\left(\frac{\alpha\delta}{\gamma} - \beta\right)t\right)\right). \tag{25}$$

It is obvious, that for

$$\boxed{\frac{\alpha\delta}{\gamma} - \beta < 0} \tag{26}$$

the path converges to

$$\widehat{\theta}_{A=D} = \bar{\theta} + \frac{\frac{\alpha\varepsilon}{\gamma}D}{\frac{\alpha\delta}{\gamma} - \beta}. \tag{44}$$

If condition (26) would not apply, fundamentals would grow or decrease infinitely depending on the initial fundamental state at $A = D$. Since an infinite expansion is economically not reasonable we apply the parameter restriction.

The convergence point is only accessible, if it's in the interval defined by the control restriction (cf. 37), i.e. $\left[\bar{\theta} + \frac{\varepsilon}{\delta}D + \frac{\gamma}{\delta}(\bar{r} - R), \bar{\theta} + \frac{\varepsilon}{\delta}D + \frac{\gamma}{\delta}\bar{r}\right]$. In other words, the convergence point is between the attack ZMLs $\left[\theta^{A=D}_{\dot{A}=0,R}, \theta^{A=D}_{\dot{A}=0,0}\right]$. Therefore, it is necessary that $\bar{\theta} + \frac{\frac{\alpha\varepsilon}{\gamma}D}{\frac{\alpha\delta}{\gamma}-\beta} > \bar{\theta} + \frac{\varepsilon}{\delta}D + \frac{\gamma}{\delta}(\bar{r} - R)$. Hence, the convergence point is feasible, if

$$R > \bar{r} - \frac{\varepsilon D}{\left(\frac{\alpha\delta}{\beta} - \gamma\right)}. \tag{45}$$

On the other side of the interval it is necessary that $\bar{\theta} + \frac{\frac{\alpha\varepsilon}{\gamma}D}{\frac{\alpha\delta}{\gamma}-\beta} < \bar{\theta} + \frac{\varepsilon}{\delta}D + \frac{\gamma}{\delta}\bar{r} \leftrightarrow \frac{\beta\delta\varepsilon D}{\gamma\left(\frac{\alpha\delta}{\gamma}-\beta\right)} < \bar{r}$, which is true (cf. condition 26). From (44) it is obvious that the maximum of $\widehat{\theta}_{A=D}$ is $\bar{\theta}$ for $D = 0$. Therefore $\widehat{\theta}_{A=D}$ is between the attack ZML of defense policy $\theta^{A=D}_{\dot{A}=0,R}$ and the no stress steady state $\bar{\theta}$.

Proof of proposition 4: we proof by contradiction and show that the intersection of the defense policy ZMLs (40) and (42) violates the state restriction (20). That is $\bar{\theta} + \frac{\alpha}{\beta}(\bar{r} - R) \neq \bar{\theta} + \frac{\gamma}{\delta}(\bar{r} - R) + \frac{\varepsilon}{\delta}A$, for $A \in [0, D]$. Reorganizing gives: $\frac{1}{\varepsilon}\left(\frac{\alpha\delta}{\beta} - \gamma\right)(\bar{r} - R) \neq A$. The left hand side is positive ($R > \bar{r}$). With the restriction to feasible convergence points (cf. proposition 3), i.e. $R > \bar{r} - \frac{\varepsilon D}{\frac{\alpha\delta}{\beta}-\gamma}$ it follows that $A > D$. Therefore, the defense policy ZMLs intersect above the defensive measure.

Proof of proposition 5: when the central bank chooses to preserve the attack in no stress ($\dot{A} = 0$ and $A = 0$), the fundamentals evolve according to

$$\theta(t) = \theta_S \exp\left(\left(\frac{\alpha\delta}{\gamma} - \beta\right)t\right) + \bar{\theta}\left(1 - \exp\left(\left(\frac{\alpha\delta}{\gamma} - \beta\right)t\right)\right). \tag{27}$$

For $\frac{\alpha\delta}{\gamma} - \beta$ (condition 26) it is obvious that the path converges to

$$\widehat{\theta}_{A=0} = \bar{\theta}.$$

The position of the no stress convergence point $\widehat{\theta}_{A=0}$ is between the fundamental ZMLs of expansion policy and defense policy. It is obvious that $\theta_{\dot{\theta}=0,R} < \widehat{\theta}_{A=0} < \theta_{\dot{\theta}=0,0}$, i.e. $\bar{\theta} - \frac{\alpha}{\beta}(R - \bar{r}) < \bar{\theta} < \bar{\theta} + \frac{\alpha}{\beta}\bar{r}$.

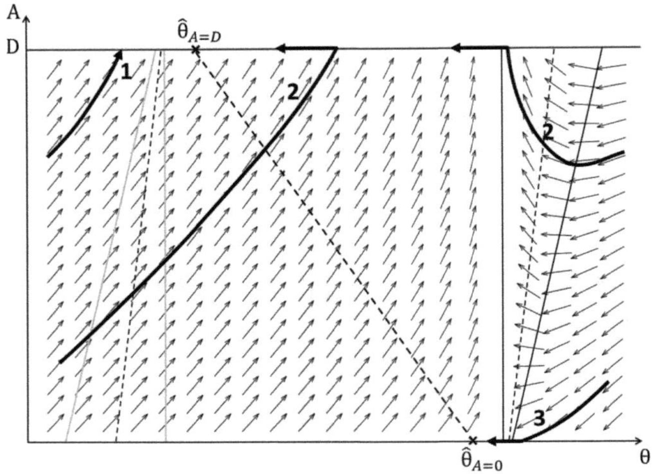

(a) expansion policy

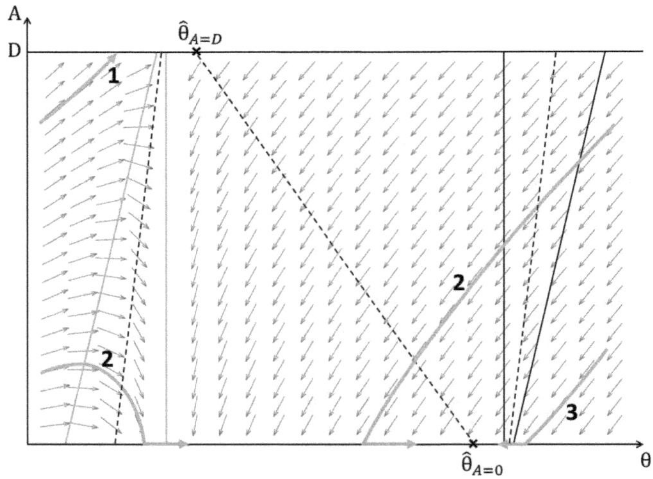

(b) defense policy

Figure I.13.: **Vector fields:** The figures show vectors that represent the directional motion of the system under expansion (black, panel a) and defense (gray, panel b). The black lines are sample trajectories, with initial values corresponding to areas 1 to 3 of figure I.8. Also shown are the ZMLs (expansion: solid black; defense: solid gray), focal points, and the identity lines (dahed black).

5.3.3. Optimal Behavior

Proof of proposition 6: the identity line is derived from equating the slopes of the paths of expansion and defense policy. For positive slopes of the trajectories we have $\frac{dA_{r=0}}{d\theta_{r=0}} = \frac{dA_{r=R}}{d\theta_{r=R}}$, while for slopes of differing sign we have $\frac{dA_{r=0}}{d\theta_{r=0}} = -\frac{dA_{r=R}}{d\theta_{r=R}}$. These equalities are equal to $\frac{\dot{A}_{r=0}}{\dot{\theta}_{r=0}} = \frac{\dot{A}_{r=R}}{\dot{\theta}_{r=R}}$ and $\frac{\dot{A}_{r=0}}{\dot{\theta}_{r=0}} = -\frac{\dot{A}_{r=R}}{\dot{\theta}_{r=R}}$. Inserting the differential equations (17) in the positive slopes, we get:

$$\frac{\gamma\bar{r} - \delta\left(\theta_S - \bar{\theta}\right) + \varepsilon A_S}{\alpha\bar{r} - \beta\left(\theta_S - \bar{\theta}\right)} = \frac{-\gamma\left(R - \bar{r}\right) - \delta\left(\theta_S - \bar{\theta}\right) + \varepsilon A_S}{-\alpha\left(R - \bar{r}\right) - \beta\left(\theta_S - \bar{\theta}\right)}.$$

Reorganizing

$$\frac{\alpha\bar{r} - \beta\left(\theta_S - \bar{\theta}\right) - \alpha R}{\alpha\bar{r} - \beta\left(\theta_S - \bar{\theta}\right)} = \frac{\gamma\bar{r} - \delta\left(\theta_S - \bar{\theta}\right) + \varepsilon A_S - \gamma R}{\gamma\bar{r} - \delta\left(\theta_S - \bar{\theta}\right) + \varepsilon A_S}$$

cancelling down

$$\frac{\alpha}{\gamma} = \frac{\alpha\bar{r} - \beta\left(\theta_S - \bar{\theta}\right)}{\gamma\bar{r} - \delta\left(\theta_S - \bar{\theta}\right) + \varepsilon A_S}$$

and solving for A_S gives the identity line:

$$\boxed{A_S = \left(\theta_S - \bar{\theta}\right)\frac{\alpha\delta - \beta\gamma}{\alpha\varepsilon} = \left(\theta_S - \bar{\theta}\right)\frac{\frac{\alpha\delta}{\gamma} - \beta}{\frac{\alpha\varepsilon}{\gamma}}.} \tag{28}$$

The function describes a straight line with negative slope in the θ, A space. The line crosses certain prominent points that are relevant for the characterization of the dynamics. The identity lines are plotted in figure I.5 on page 30.

If $A_S = 0$, then $\theta_S = \bar{\theta} = \widehat{\theta}_{A=0}$; if $A_S = D$ then $\theta_S = \bar{\theta} + \frac{\frac{\alpha\varepsilon}{\gamma}D}{\frac{\alpha\delta}{\gamma} - \beta} = \widehat{\theta}_{A=D}$. Inserting in the attack ZML (43) for expansion policy gives: $\theta_S = \bar{\theta} + \frac{\gamma}{\delta}\bar{r} + \frac{\varepsilon}{\delta}\left(\theta_S - \bar{\theta}\right)\frac{\frac{\alpha\delta}{\gamma} - \beta}{\frac{\alpha\varepsilon}{\gamma}}$ and solving for θ_S gives: $\bar{\theta} + \frac{\alpha}{\beta}\bar{r}$. Using (42) for defense policy we get: $\theta_S = \bar{\theta} - \frac{\gamma}{\delta}\left(R - \bar{r}\right) + \frac{\varepsilon}{\delta}\left(\theta_S - \bar{\theta}\right)\frac{\frac{\alpha\delta}{\gamma} - \beta}{\frac{\alpha\varepsilon}{\gamma}}$ and solving for θ_S gives: $\bar{\theta} + \frac{\alpha}{\beta}\left(\bar{r} - R\right)$. Thus, the identity line crosses the intersection of the defense ZMLs, the upper and lower convergence points and the intersection of the expansion ZMLs.

To proof, which policy has a higher slope above the identity line we add a small $\xi > 0$ to the attack value, $A_S + \xi = \left(\theta_S - \bar{\theta}\right)\frac{\frac{\alpha\delta}{\gamma} - \beta}{\frac{\alpha\varepsilon}{\gamma}} + \xi$. We then proof that expansion policy has a higher slope than defense policy above the identity line. Therefore, it is necessary that:

$$\frac{\dot{A}_{r=0}}{\dot{\theta}_{r=0}}\left(\theta_S, A_S + \xi\right) > \frac{\dot{A}_{r=R}}{\dot{\theta}_{r=R}}\left(\theta_S, A_S + \xi\right)$$

$$\frac{\gamma\bar{r}-\delta\left(\theta_S-\bar{\theta}\right)+\varepsilon\left(\left(\theta_S-\bar{\theta}\right)\frac{\alpha\delta-\beta\gamma}{\alpha\varepsilon}+\xi\right)}{\alpha\bar{r}-\beta\left(\theta_S-\bar{\theta}\right)} > \frac{-\gamma\left(R-\bar{r}\right)-\delta\left(\theta_S-\bar{\theta}\right)+\varepsilon\left(\left(\theta_S-\bar{\theta}\right)\frac{\alpha\delta-\beta\gamma}{\alpha\varepsilon}+\xi\right)}{-\alpha\left(R-\bar{r}\right)-\beta\left(\theta_S-\bar{\theta}\right)}.$$

Depending on the location in the state space the directional movement of the fundamentals and the attack differs. The identity line derived is valid in areas where the slopes of the trajectories have positive signs. That is to the left of the attack ZML of defense policy, between the fundamental ZMLs and to the right of the attack ZML of expansion policy. Since the directions of the differential equations differ across these areas, we proof the inequality by cases.

1. To the left of the attack ZML of defense policy both trajectories have the same direction, with $\dot{\theta}_{r=0}$, $\dot{A}_{r=0}$, $\dot{\theta}_{r=R}$, $\dot{A}_{r=R} > 0$. Therefore, we rearrange the inequality as follows:

$$\begin{aligned}
\frac{-\alpha\left(R-\bar{r}\right)-\beta\left(\theta_S-\bar{\theta}\right)}{\alpha\bar{r}-\beta\left(\theta_S-\bar{\theta}\right)} &> \frac{-\gamma\left(R-\bar{r}\right)-\delta\left(\theta_S-\bar{\theta}\right)+\varepsilon\left(\left(\theta_S-\bar{\theta}\right)\frac{\alpha\delta-\beta\gamma}{\alpha\varepsilon}+\xi\right)}{\gamma\bar{r}-\delta\left(\theta_S-\bar{\theta}\right)+\varepsilon\left(\left(\theta_S-\bar{\theta}\right)\frac{\alpha\delta-\beta\gamma}{\alpha\varepsilon}+\xi\right)}\\
1-\frac{\alpha R}{\alpha\bar{r}-\beta\left(\theta_S-\bar{\theta}\right)} &> 1-\frac{\gamma R}{\gamma\bar{r}-\delta\left(\theta_S-\bar{\theta}\right)+\varepsilon\left(\left(\theta_S-\bar{\theta}\right)\frac{\alpha\delta-\beta\gamma}{\alpha\varepsilon}+\xi\right)}\\
\frac{\alpha}{\alpha\bar{r}-\beta\left(\theta_S-\bar{\theta}\right)} &< \frac{\gamma}{\gamma\bar{r}-\delta\left(\theta_S-\bar{\theta}\right)+\varepsilon\left(\left(\theta_S-\bar{\theta}\right)\frac{\alpha\delta-\beta\gamma}{\alpha\varepsilon}+\xi\right)}\\
\frac{\alpha}{\gamma} &< \frac{\alpha\bar{r}-\beta\left(\theta_S-\bar{\theta}\right)}{\gamma\bar{r}-\delta\left(\theta_S-\bar{\theta}\right)+\varepsilon\left(\left(\theta_S-\bar{\theta}\right)\frac{\alpha\delta-\beta\gamma}{\alpha\varepsilon}+\xi\right)},
\end{aligned}$$

which is false, since $\frac{\alpha}{\gamma}=\frac{\alpha\bar{r}-\beta\left(\theta_S-\bar{\theta}\right)}{\gamma\bar{r}-\delta\left(\theta_S-\bar{\theta}\right)+\varepsilon A_S}$ (cf. equation 28). Consequently, the expansion policy trajectory has the higher slope to the left of the attack ZML for $0 \leq A \leq D$.

2. Between the fundamental ZMLs both trajectories move in opposite directions, with $\dot{\theta}_{r=0}$, $\dot{A}_{r=0} > 0$ and $\dot{\theta}_{r=R}$, $\dot{A}_{r=R} < 0$. Hence,

$$\begin{aligned}
\frac{-\alpha\left(R-\bar{r}\right)-\beta\left(\theta_S-\bar{\theta}\right)}{\alpha\bar{r}-\beta\left(\theta_S-\bar{\theta}\right)} &< \frac{-\gamma\left(R-\bar{r}\right)-\delta\left(\theta_S-\bar{\theta}\right)+\varepsilon\left(\left(\theta_S-\bar{\theta}\right)\frac{\alpha\delta-\beta\gamma}{\alpha\varepsilon}+\xi\right)}{\gamma\bar{r}-\delta\left(\theta_S-\bar{\theta}\right)+\varepsilon\left(\left(\theta_S-\bar{\theta}\right)\frac{\alpha\delta-\beta\gamma}{\alpha\varepsilon}+\xi\right)}\\
1-\frac{\alpha R}{\alpha\bar{r}-\beta\left(\theta_S-\bar{\theta}\right)} &< 1-\frac{\gamma R}{\gamma\bar{r}-\delta\left(\theta_S-\bar{\theta}\right)+\varepsilon\left(\left(\theta_S-\bar{\theta}\right)\frac{\alpha\delta-\beta\gamma}{\alpha\varepsilon}+\xi\right)}\\
\frac{\alpha}{\alpha\bar{r}-\beta\left(\theta_S-\bar{\theta}\right)} &> \frac{\gamma}{\gamma\bar{r}-\delta\left(\theta_S-\bar{\theta}\right)+\varepsilon\left(\left(\theta_S-\bar{\theta}\right)\frac{\alpha\delta-\beta\gamma}{\alpha\varepsilon}+\xi\right)}\\
\frac{\alpha}{\gamma} &> \frac{\alpha\bar{r}-\beta\left(\theta_S-\bar{\theta}\right)}{\gamma\bar{r}-\delta\left(\theta_S-\bar{\theta}\right)+\varepsilon\left(\left(\theta_S-\bar{\theta}\right)\frac{\alpha\delta-\beta\gamma}{\alpha\varepsilon}+\xi\right)},
\end{aligned}$$

which is true, confirming that above the identity line and between the fundamental ZMLs expansion policy leads to a higher slope, while below defense policy leads to a higher slope.

3. To the right of the attack ZML of expansion policy both trajectories again have the same direction, with $\dot{\theta}_{r=0}$, $\dot{A}_{r=0}$, $\dot{\theta}_{r=R}$, $\dot{A}_{r=R} < 0$. Hence,

$$\begin{aligned}
\frac{-\alpha(R-\bar{r})-\beta\left(\theta_S-\bar{\theta}\right)}{\alpha\bar{r}-\beta\left(\theta_S-\bar{\theta}\right)} &> \frac{-\gamma(R-\bar{r})-\delta\left(\theta_S-\bar{\theta}\right)+\varepsilon\left(\left(\theta_S-\bar{\theta}\right)\frac{\alpha\delta-\beta\gamma}{\alpha\varepsilon}+\xi\right)}{\gamma\bar{r}-\delta\left(\theta_S-\bar{\theta}\right)+\varepsilon\left(\left(\theta_S-\bar{\theta}\right)\frac{\alpha\delta-\beta\gamma}{\alpha\varepsilon}+\xi\right)}\\
1-\frac{\alpha R}{\alpha\bar{r}-\beta\left(\theta_S-\bar{\theta}\right)} &> 1-\frac{\gamma R}{\gamma\bar{r}-\delta\left(\theta_S-\bar{\theta}\right)+\varepsilon\left(\left(\theta_S-\bar{\theta}\right)\frac{\alpha\delta-\beta\gamma}{\alpha\varepsilon}+\xi\right)}\\
\frac{\alpha}{\alpha\bar{r}-\beta\left(\theta_S-\bar{\theta}\right)} &< \frac{\gamma}{\gamma\bar{r}-\delta\left(\theta_S-\bar{\theta}\right)+\varepsilon\left(\left(\theta_S-\bar{\theta}\right)\frac{\alpha\delta-\beta\gamma}{\alpha\varepsilon}+\xi\right)}\\
\frac{\alpha}{\gamma} &> \frac{\alpha\bar{r}-\beta\left(\theta_S-\bar{\theta}\right)}{\gamma\bar{r}-\delta\left(\theta_S-\bar{\theta}\right)+\varepsilon\left(\left(\theta_S-\bar{\theta}\right)\frac{\alpha\delta-\beta\gamma}{\alpha\varepsilon}+\xi\right)},
\end{aligned}$$

which is false, since $\dot{\theta}_{r=0} = \alpha\bar{r}-\beta\left(\theta_S-\bar{\theta}\right) < 0$ and $\dot{A}_{r=0} = \gamma\bar{r}-\delta\left(\theta_S-\bar{\theta}\right) + \varepsilon\left(\left(\theta_S-\bar{\theta}\right)\frac{\alpha\delta-\beta\gamma}{\alpha\varepsilon}\right) < 0$. This confirms that the trajectory of defense policy has the higher slope to the right of the attack ZML of expansion policy for $0 \leq A \leq D$.

To find the identity line, we compared the slopes of the directional movement in the θ, A space. The identity line considered resulted from a positive slope of the trajectories of expansion and defense policy. In the state space between the expansion policy ZMLs and the defense policy ZMLs the slopes of the trajectories have a different sign (cf. figure I.3). Therefore, there are two more identity lines given by

$$\frac{\dot{A}_{r=0}}{\dot{\theta}_{r=0}} = -\frac{\dot{A}_{r=R}}{\dot{\theta}_{r=R}}.$$

Inserting the differential equations (17)

$$\frac{\gamma\bar{r}-\delta\left(\theta_S-\bar{\theta}\right)+\varepsilon A_S}{\alpha\bar{r}-\beta\left(\theta_S-\bar{\theta}\right)} = -\frac{-\gamma(R-\bar{r})-\delta\left(\theta_S-\bar{\theta}\right)+\varepsilon A_S}{-\alpha(R-\bar{r})-\beta\left(\theta_S-\bar{\theta}\right)}$$

and rearranging

$$\frac{\alpha\bar{r}-\beta\left(\theta_S-\bar{\theta}\right)-\alpha R}{\alpha\bar{r}-\beta\left(\theta_S-\bar{\theta}\right)} = \frac{-\gamma\bar{r}+\delta\left(\theta_S-\bar{\theta}\right)-\varepsilon A_S+\gamma R}{\gamma\bar{r}-\delta\left(\theta_S-\bar{\theta}\right)+\varepsilon A_S}$$

gives

$$1-\frac{\alpha R}{\alpha\bar{r}-\beta\left(\theta_S-\bar{\theta}\right)} = -1+\frac{\gamma R}{\gamma\bar{r}-\delta\left(\theta_S-\bar{\theta}\right)+\varepsilon A_S}$$

or

$$2 = \frac{\gamma R}{\gamma \bar{r} - \delta\left(\theta_S - \bar{\theta}\right) + \varepsilon A_S} + \frac{\alpha R}{\alpha \bar{r} - \beta\left(\theta_S - \bar{\theta}\right)}.$$

Which can be solved for A_S

$$\boxed{A_S = -\frac{1}{\varepsilon}\left(\gamma \bar{r} - \delta\left(\theta_S - \bar{\theta}\right) + \frac{\gamma R\left(\alpha \bar{r} - \beta\left(\theta_S - \bar{\theta}\right)\right)}{\alpha R - 2\left(\alpha \bar{r} - \beta\left(\theta_S - \bar{\theta}\right)\right)}\right).} \tag{28}$$

Which is a function that defines two curves with positive slopes in the feasible attack space. The curves cross the intersection of the defense policy ZMLs and the expansion policy ZMLs. Again, we are interested, whether expansion policy has a higher slope above the identity line $(A_S + \xi)$. To compare the absolute value of the slope we consider only positive slopes. Since the direction of the motion changes, depending on the state, we have to proof by cases.

1. Between the defense policy ZMLs the differential equations have the following signs: $\dot{\theta}_{r=0},\ \dot{A}_{r=0} > 0$ and $\dot{\theta}_{r=R} > 0,\ \dot{A}_{r=R} < 0$. Therefore, we get:

$$\frac{\dot{A}_{r=0}}{\dot{\theta}_{r=0}}\left(A_S + \xi\right) > -\frac{\dot{A}_{r=R}}{\dot{\theta}_{r=R}}\left(A_S + \xi\right)$$

after inserting, we get

$$\frac{\gamma \bar{r} - \delta\left(\theta_S - \bar{\theta}\right) + \varepsilon\left(-\frac{1}{\varepsilon}\left(\gamma \bar{r} - \delta\left(\theta_S - \bar{\theta}\right) + \frac{\gamma R\left(\alpha \bar{r} - \beta\left(\theta_S - \bar{\theta}\right)\right)}{\alpha R - 2\left(\alpha \bar{r} - \beta\left(\theta_S - \bar{\theta}\right)\right)}\right) + \xi\right)}{\alpha \bar{r} - \beta\left(\theta_S - \bar{\theta}\right)} >$$
$$-\frac{-\gamma\left(R - \bar{r}\right) - \delta\left(\theta_S - \bar{\theta}\right) + \varepsilon\left(-\frac{1}{\varepsilon}\left(\gamma \bar{r} - \delta\left(\theta_S - \bar{\theta}\right) + \frac{\gamma R\left(\alpha \bar{r} - \beta\left(\theta_S - \bar{\theta}\right)\right)}{\alpha R - 2\left(\alpha \bar{r} - \beta\left(\theta_S - \bar{\theta}\right)\right)}\right) + \xi\right)}{-\alpha\left(R - \bar{r}\right) - \beta\left(\theta_S - \bar{\theta}\right)},$$

$$\frac{-\alpha\left(R - \bar{r}\right) - \beta\left(\theta_S - \bar{\theta}\right)}{\alpha \bar{r} - \beta\left(\theta_S - \bar{\theta}\right)} >$$
$$-\frac{-\gamma\left(R - \bar{r}\right) - \delta\left(\theta_S - \bar{\theta}\right) + \varepsilon\left(-\frac{1}{\varepsilon}\left(\gamma \bar{r} - \delta\left(\theta_S - \bar{\theta}\right) + \frac{\gamma R\left(\alpha \bar{r} - \beta\left(\theta_S - \bar{\theta}\right)\right)}{\alpha R - 2\left(\alpha \bar{r} - \beta\left(\theta_S - \bar{\theta}\right)\right)}\right) + \xi\right)}{\gamma \bar{r} - \delta\left(\theta_S - \bar{\theta}\right) + \varepsilon\left(-\frac{1}{\varepsilon}\left(\gamma \bar{r} - \delta\left(\theta_S - \bar{\theta}\right) + \frac{\gamma R\left(\alpha \bar{r} - \beta\left(\theta_S - \bar{\theta}\right)\right)}{\alpha R - 2\left(\alpha \bar{r} - \beta\left(\theta_S - \bar{\theta}\right)\right)}\right) + \xi\right)},$$

$$1-\frac{\alpha R}{\alpha\bar{r}-\beta\left(\theta_S-\bar{\theta}\right)}>$$
$$-1+\frac{\gamma R}{\gamma\bar{r}-\delta\left(\theta_S-\bar{\theta}\right)+\varepsilon\left(-\frac{1}{\varepsilon}\left(\gamma\bar{r}-\delta\left(\theta_S-\bar{\theta}\right)+\frac{\gamma R\left(\alpha\bar{r}-\beta\left(\theta_S-\bar{\theta}\right)\right)}{\alpha R-2\left(\alpha\bar{r}-\beta\left(\theta_S-\bar{\theta}\right)\right)}\right)+\xi\right)},$$

$$2>\frac{\gamma R}{\gamma\bar{r}-\delta\left(\theta_S-\bar{\theta}\right)+\varepsilon\left(-\frac{1}{\varepsilon}\left(\gamma\bar{r}-\delta\left(\theta_S-\bar{\theta}\right)+\frac{\gamma R\left(\alpha\bar{r}-\beta\left(\theta_S-\bar{\theta}\right)\right)}{\alpha R-2\left(\alpha\bar{r}-\beta\left(\theta_S-\bar{\theta}\right)\right)}\right)+\xi\right)}$$
$$+\frac{\alpha R}{\alpha\bar{r}-\beta\left(\theta_S-\bar{\theta}\right)},$$

which is true, since $2=\frac{\gamma R}{\gamma\bar{r}-\delta\left(\theta_S-\bar{\theta}\right)+\varepsilon A_S}+\frac{\alpha R}{\alpha\bar{r}-\beta\left(\theta_S-\bar{\theta}\right)}$ (cf. equation 28). Hence, above the identity line expansion policy leads to the higher slope of the state trajectory.

2. Between the expansion policy ZMLs the differential equations have the following signs: $\dot{\theta}_{r=0}<0$, $\dot{A}_{r=0}>0$ and $\dot{\theta}_{r=R}$, $\dot{A}_{r=R}<0$. To compare positive slopes of the trajectories in this area we write

$$-\frac{\dot{A}_{r=0}}{\dot{\theta}_{r=0}}\left(A_S+\xi\right)>\frac{\dot{A}_{r=R}}{\dot{\theta}_{r=R}}\left(A_S+\xi\right).$$

after inserting, we get

$$-\frac{\gamma\bar{r}-\delta\left(\theta_S-\bar{\theta}\right)+\varepsilon\left(-\frac{1}{\varepsilon}\left(\gamma\bar{r}-\delta\left(\theta_S-\bar{\theta}\right)+\frac{\gamma R\left(\alpha\bar{r}-\beta\left(\theta_S-\bar{\theta}\right)\right)}{\alpha R-2\left(\alpha\bar{r}-\beta\left(\theta_S-\bar{\theta}\right)\right)}\right)+\xi\right)}{\alpha\bar{r}-\beta\left(\theta_S-\bar{\theta}\right)}>$$
$$\frac{-\gamma\left(R-\bar{r}\right)-\delta\left(\theta_S-\bar{\theta}\right)+\varepsilon\left(-\frac{1}{\varepsilon}\left(\gamma\bar{r}-\delta\left(\theta_S-\bar{\theta}\right)+\frac{\gamma R\left(\alpha\bar{r}-\beta\left(\theta_S-\bar{\theta}\right)\right)}{\alpha R-2\left(\alpha\bar{r}-\beta\left(\theta_S-\bar{\theta}\right)\right)}\right)+\xi\right)}{-\alpha\left(R-\bar{r}\right)-\beta\left(\theta_S-\bar{\theta}\right)}.$$

$$-\frac{-\alpha\left(R-\bar{r}\right)-\beta\left(\theta_S-\bar{\theta}\right)}{\alpha\bar{r}-\beta\left(\theta_S-\bar{\theta}\right)}<$$
$$\frac{-\gamma\left(R-\bar{r}\right)-\delta\left(\theta_S-\bar{\theta}\right)+\varepsilon\left(-\frac{1}{\varepsilon}\left(\gamma\bar{r}-\delta\left(\theta_S-\bar{\theta}\right)+\frac{\gamma R\left(\alpha\bar{r}-\beta\left(\theta_S-\bar{\theta}\right)\right)}{\alpha R-2\left(\alpha\bar{r}-\beta\left(\theta_S-\bar{\theta}\right)\right)}\right)+\xi\right)}{\gamma\bar{r}-\delta\left(\theta_S-\bar{\theta}\right)+\varepsilon\left(-\frac{1}{\varepsilon}\left(\gamma\bar{r}-\delta\left(\theta_S-\bar{\theta}\right)+\frac{\gamma R\left(\alpha\bar{r}-\beta\left(\theta_S-\bar{\theta}\right)\right)}{\alpha R-2\left(\alpha\bar{r}-\beta\left(\theta_S-\bar{\theta}\right)\right)}\right)+\xi\right)},$$

$$-1+\frac{\alpha R}{\alpha\bar{r}-\beta\left(\theta_S-\bar{\theta}\right)}<$$
$$1-\frac{\gamma R}{\gamma\bar{r}-\delta\left(\theta_S-\bar{\theta}\right)+\varepsilon\left(-\frac{1}{\varepsilon}\left(\gamma\bar{r}-\delta\left(\theta_S-\bar{\theta}\right)+\frac{\gamma R\left(\alpha\bar{r}-\beta\left(\theta_S-\bar{\theta}\right)\right)}{\alpha R-2\left(\alpha\bar{r}-\beta\left(\theta_S-\bar{\theta}\right)\right)}\right)+\xi\right)},$$

$$\frac{\gamma R}{\gamma\bar{r}-\delta\left(\theta_S-\bar{\theta}\right)+\varepsilon\left(-\frac{1}{\varepsilon}\left(\gamma\bar{r}-\delta\left(\theta_S-\bar{\theta}\right)+\frac{\gamma R\left(\alpha\bar{r}-\beta\left(\theta_S-\bar{\theta}\right)\right)}{\alpha R-2\left(\alpha\bar{r}-\beta\left(\theta_S-\bar{\theta}\right)\right)}\right)+\xi\right)}$$
$$+\frac{\alpha R}{\alpha\bar{r}-\beta\left(\theta_S-\bar{\theta}\right)}<2,$$

which is true, since $2=\frac{\gamma R}{\gamma\bar{r}-\delta\left(\theta_S-\bar{\theta}\right)+\varepsilon A_S}+\frac{\alpha R}{\alpha\bar{r}-\beta\left(\theta_S-\bar{\theta}\right)}$ (cf. equation 28). Therefore, above the identity line, expansion policy leads to the higher slope, whereas, below defense policy has the higher slope.

The identity lines and the areas with the respective higher slope are plotted in figure I.5 on page 30.

Proof of proposition 11: we give a condition for which the value of an immediate opt-out is better than the value of converging in high stress:

$$\frac{\theta_S-c}{\rho}>\int_0^{\infty}\exp\left(-\rho t\right)\left(\left(\theta_S-\widehat{\theta}_{A=D}\right)\exp\left(\left(\frac{\alpha\delta}{\gamma}-\beta\right)t\right)+\widehat{\theta}_{A=D}\right)dt$$

$$\frac{\theta_S-c}{\rho}>-\frac{\theta_S-\widehat{\theta}_{A=D}}{\frac{\alpha\delta}{\gamma}-\beta-\rho}+\frac{\widehat{\theta}_{A=D}}{\rho}$$

Rearranging and solving for θ_S gives:

$$\theta_S>\widehat{\theta}_{A=D}+c\frac{\frac{\alpha\delta}{\gamma}-\beta-\rho}{\frac{\alpha\delta}{\gamma}-\beta}$$

$$\boxed{\theta_c\equiv\widehat{\theta}_{A=D}+c\frac{\frac{\alpha\delta}{\gamma}-\beta-\rho}{\frac{\alpha\delta}{\gamma}-\beta}.}$$

Part II.

The Mispricing of Debt—Influences of Ratings on Coordination

1. Introduction

In financing an investment project a firm can resort to internal or external funding. To get good financing conditions the firm, if solvent, will disclose abundant information about its fundamental state, cash flows, assets, liabilities etc. If not solvent, the firm has an incentive to hide as much as it can or give a wrong assessment about its fundamental state. In any case the firm's information is superior compared to those of investors.

To support functioning capital markets, governmental laws on accounting and disclosure aim on protection of investors and comparability between firms. Besides governmental regulation, credit rating agencies publish their own assessment of the creditworthiness of securities to facilitate financing decisions. Whether a project is a success for the firm and the investors depends on the actions of both parties. That is, the investors do not foreclose prior to maturity and the firm responsibly invests the provided capital. This paper focuses on the strategic uncertainty faced by investors. Thereby, an investor does not know what other investors know about the firm. If an investor thinks that other investors have a bad assessment about the firm and believes that other investors foreclose, it might be best to also foreclose independent of the actual fundamental state.

To form beliefs and make decisions, investors use two sources of information: public and private information. Public information is common to all investors, whereas private information is idiosyncratic, implying dispersed beliefs among investors. A rating is an additional source of public information that serves as a coordination device for investors' beliefs. Compared to other public information, ratings have the advantage to be easy understood, due to the categorization in notches. Ashcraft et al. (2011) note that the visibility of the rating provides information to less informed investors. Since regulation of capital requirements refers to ratings—changes that induce regulatory arbitrage affect security prices. Boot et al. (2006) add, that credit ratings are especially valuable through their monitoring role. From this point of view, ratings are a useful and much appreciated tool in financing decisions.

However, the subprime crisis changed the view on the role of the credit rating agencies. The literature discusses the influences of competition, reputation, and the payment model of rating agencies.

Skreta and Veldkamp (2009) model a market in which issuers can choose between ratings offered by the agencies. They show that with increasing complexity in assets, ratings differ sufficiently to provide an incentive to shop for ratings. In a model of competition between rating agencies Bolton et al. (2012) find that increasing competition allows to shop for ratings. A view that is also held in an early paper by Cantor and Packer (1994). In boom times mistakes by rating agencies have less influence and investors are more inattentive so that rating agencies may be inclined to inflate ratings. He et al. (2011) observe that especially MBS emitted by the large issuers received more AAA ratings than emissions by small issuers. This gap widened with the credit market booming and consequently resulted in more rapidly declining prices of MBS of large issuers during the crisis.

Ashcraft et al. (2011) observe a correlation between ratings and MBS yield spreads and raise the question whether this is caused by either valuable information obtained through the credit rating agency or categorization of letter ratings, mistakes, or biases.

Faure-Grimaud et al. (2009) show, in a model of competition between rating agencies, that if rated firms are uncertain about the underlying state and the mandate is not observable, competition among credit rating agencies leads to less information. In Opp et al. (2013) the rating agency stops acquiring information for investment grade securities and simply inflates ratings.

Griffin and Tang (2011) compare the assessments of divisions in a respective credit rating agency for the CDO market. The rating team is in contact with and acquires clients. It also gives the initial rating, while the surveillance team monitors afterwards. Griffin and Tang find that the surveillance teams—less influenced by conflicts of interest—calculated more accurately, estimated higher default correlations, and calculated collateral quality more pessimistic than the rating teams.

Mathis et al. (2009) model the reputation of credit rating agencies and find that during depressions rating agencies build up reputation, which they put at stake in boom times, until a crisis emerges and reputation falls down.

In Boot et al. (2006) the credit quality of a firm can take three states: bad, neutral, and good. In the bad case the firm can invest in a recovery effort to restore neutral credit quality. The firm can engage in a low risk and a high risk project to pay its debt. Institutional investors are only allowed for investment grade firms. Boot et al. show that if a large enough fraction of institutional investors act according to the issued rating, other investors follow, thus resolving multiple equilibria and moral hazard. Through the credit watch procedure, that includes the recovery effort into the rating, the rating agency adds new information to the market.

As a response to the financial crisis the European Parliament (2013) adopted a co-decision, that prompts banks to do their own risk assessment, allows unsolicited ratings of government bonds only at certain dates, and makes rating agencies accountable for errors. Moreover till 2020 references to ratings will be canceled from EU law. This view is supported by scholars, who state that "safety judgments should remain the responsibility of the regulated institutions themselves, with oversight by regulators" (White, 2010). Besides, it is rather astonishing that the credit rating agencies had the 'force of law' when one has a look at their disclaimers. Standard and Poors (2013) for example state: "Credit ratings issued by Ratings Services are solely statements of opinion and not statements of fact or recommendations to purchase, hold, or sell any securities or make any other investment decisions."[33]

The literature on stock price effects due to rating changes can be briefly summarized in that it is commonly observed that prices react strongly to downgrades but not significantly to upgrades (cf. Ederington and Goh, 1993). Dichev and Piotroski (2001) confirm the pattern that prices react strongly to downgrades, especially for low credit quality. Moreover they observe subsequent losses in the stock price if a downgrade is followed by a report of earning losses. When the current rating is added as explanatory variable, Jorion and Zhang (2007) find that the current rating explains the difference in effects of upgrades and downgrades. The effect of an upgrade is especially important for low grade firms and the investment grade barrier becomes insignificant.

Morris and Shin (2004) transfer the global game approach to a debt contract where investors face strategic uncertainty. Sufficiently precise private information ensures equilibrium uniqueness and allows to derive a price of debt and identify the price effect of coordination. They find that neglecting the coordination effect leads to an overpricing of debt that increases with risk. Carlson and Hale (2006) find that including a rating increases the likelihood of multiple equilibria and that investors' posteriors are more sensitive to unfavorable ratings.

Cornand and Heinemann (2008) state that the relative weight of public signals compared to their informational content is too high. For imprecise information, coordination can lead to substantial deviations from fundamentals. Hence, limiting the degree of publicity conditional on precision increases welfare. In a further study Cornand and Heinemann (2009) argue that though central bank announcements are publicly observable precision remains unknown. Hence, investors' perceptions about the precision differ causing different posteriors about the state of the economy. Cornand and Heinemann conclude that the probability of multiple equilibria is reduced if a central bank discloses various imprecise signals with unknown precision.

[33]Moody's (2013) has a similar statement: "As ratings are designed exclusively for the purpose of grading obligations according to their credit quality, they should not be used alone as a basis for investment operations. For example, they have no value in forecasting the direction of future trends of market price."

In contrast, Lindner (2006) argues that investors perceive public information in reference to their private information. The central bank bases its forecast upon different variables. If it discloses these variables, investors draw different conclusions. This dispersion of beliefs reduces the probability of multiple equilibria. Edmond (2011) analyzes a coordination game where a regime is able to control information and shows that the posterior beliefs can be manipulated to reduce the probability of a regime change.

Results of the paper I extend the global game model of Morris and Shin (2004) by introducing a publicly observable rating that can be biased. The rating reduces the idiosyncratic dispersion of beliefs and allows a better coordination of investors. Due to this coordination effect, changes in public information have a higher impact on the investment decision of investors, the default point, and the forecasted bond price.

When investors observe a positively biased rating they reduce their expectations accordingly. Hence, the bias results in a higher rate of foreclosure and increases the default point.

If the bond price increases, the expected payoff of the investment turns negative and foreclosure becomes profitable. Therefore, an increase in the bond price leads to more investors foreclosing and a higher default point.

If a rating agency claims to forecast the default probability correctly, it has to acknowledge its own influence on the coordination of investors. The rating coordinates beliefs, thereby influences the mass of foreclosing investors and hence the firm's default probability conditional on publicly available information. Necessarily, a rating agency neglecting the influence of its own assessment gives a wrong rating.

With increasing relative precision of public information, multiple equilibria emerge and the stable equilibria diverge. Hence, for infinite precision of public information as well as imprecise private information, either all investors foreclose or all investors roll over. Thus, in case of multiple equilibria, the fundamental state has no impact on the equilibrium selection, only coordination matters.

The survival probability of the firm conditional on publicly available information equals the forecasted bond price. Through the concentration of beliefs and the induced increase in coordination a rating allows a more accurate pricing of debt. I show that pricing methods omitting the rating overprice bad debt and underprice good debt. Thus, omitting the rating in pricing debt rewards bad borrowers and punishes good borrowers.

2. Model

2.1. Description

A continuum of investors holds the bonds of a firm. The fractions held are equally distributed and negligible in size. If the firm survives, the repayment to investors will be R, in case of default it is zero. The state of the firm is characterized through the fundamental state θ, which is drawn from an improper uniform prior distribution and cannot be observed directly. However, public information about the firm is available $y = \theta + \eta_y$, where η_y is an error that is normally distributed with mean 0 and precision α.[34] Every investor i observes a private signal $x_i = \theta + \varepsilon_i$, where ε_i is normally distributed with mean 0 and precision β. Moreover the firm is rated and the rating $z = \theta + \eta_z$ is made publicly available. η_z is normally distributed with mean b (bias) and precision γ. The error terms $\eta_y, \varepsilon_i, \eta_z$ are independent. After receiving the information, y, x_i, z, the investors get the chance to review their investment and decide whether to foreclose or whether to role over their position. They can redeem their bond at price p. The firm is solvent if $\theta \geq 0$ and the firm is liquid if all foreclosing investors can be redeemed $\theta \geq \theta_c$, i.e. if the fundamental state exceeds a critical state.

The sequence of events in the game is as follows:

1. Investors are endowed with bonds of the firm
2. Nature draws θ
3. Public y and private x_i signals are observed
4. Rating z is issued
5. Price p, at which the bond can be redeemed, is observed
6. After observing the price and all signals, investors decide upon rollover
7. If the foreclosure rate is higher than the critical state θ_c, the firm is illiquid and the investment p is lost

The rating serves as an additional source of public information. It enhances the investor's level of information in two ways: through the signal itself and through its precision. The rating, an investor observes, is her unconditional expectation about the funda-

[34] Hence, the standard deviation of the error term is $\frac{1}{\sqrt{\alpha}}$.

mental state:

$$z|\,\theta \sim N\left(\theta + b, \frac{1}{\gamma}\right).$$

If a bias exists, the information is blurred. A rating has two types of errors: a systematic (bias) and a stochastic (precision). If the bias is observable, investors adapt their posteriors accordingly. Hence, investors will adjust their assessment according to the bias and form a conditional expectation about the fundamental state:

$$\theta|\, z \sim N\left(z - b, \frac{1}{\gamma}\right).$$

Here, bias just refers to a difference in information and not necessarily to a wrong rating. Deviations of the rating can be due to scale, timing, and assessment. Hence, securities having the same rating not necessarily bear exactly the same risk.[35] Sources for a different assessment are superior information, mistakes made in the rating process, or incentives to boost ratings. To render an outstanding reputation, however, a rating agency might be very conservative in the issuance of ratings resulting in a negative bias.

In the overall assessment, when investors form their posterior belief about the underlying state, they weigh every source of information according to its precision. Applying standard Bayesian updating gives the posterior distribution of the fundamentals:[36]

$$\theta\,|y, x_i, z \sim N\left(\frac{\alpha y + \beta x_i + \gamma\,(z-b)}{\alpha + \beta + \gamma}, \frac{1}{\alpha + \beta + \gamma}\right). \tag{1}$$

Note that the mean of the posterior can be altered through the rating itself (its mean or bias) as well as through its precision.

Even if the conditional expectation and the precision are the same as in public information ($y = z, b = 0, \alpha = \gamma$), the rating changes the posterior belief of every investor. With the rating the investors are more confident about their beliefs, i.e. the variance of the posterior is lower. Figure (II.1)[37] shows different conditional expectations used to form the posterior. For diverging information the rating can serve as a coordination devise. Boot et al. (2006) consider ratings as most valuable in this case.

Every investor uses her posterior to calculate the expected payoff. An investor rolls over if her payoff is at least zero or positive. The investment pays back money if its state

[35]The rating agencies acknowledge: "Obligations carrying the same rating are not claimed to be of absolutely equal credit quality. In a broad sense, they are alike in position, but since there are a limited number of rating classes used in grading thousands of bonds, the symbols cannot reflect the same shadings of risk which actually exist." (cf. Moody's 2013).

[36]Equation (1) applies if a bias exists. If there is no bias, then $b = 0$.

[37]For the plots I use the precision values of Morris and Shin (2004) as benchmark. Moreover I assume that the rating is more precise than public information. If not stated differently, the precision parameters are: $\alpha = 1$, $\beta = 5$ and $\gamma = 2$.

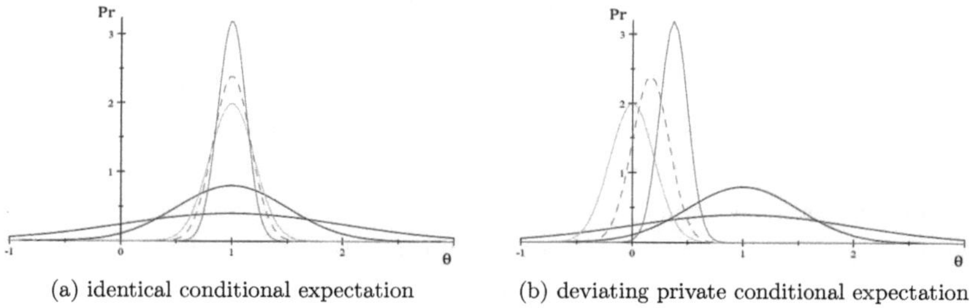

Figure II.1.: **Conditional expectations and posteriors:** Panels (a) and (b) show the conditional expectations of public information (flat black), rating (steeper black), private information (lightgray), and the resulting posterior with (gray) and without rating (dashed gray).

is better than the critical state $\theta \geq \theta_c$, in this case the payoff is $R - p$. In case of default, which is associated with states worse than the critical state $\theta < \theta_c$, repayment is zero and the investor loses her investment p. Thus, the expected payoff is

$$(R-p)\Pr(\theta \geq \theta_c \,|x_i, y, z) - p\Pr(\theta < \theta_c \,|x_i, y, z). \tag{2}$$

Normalizing the repayment to 1, the expected payoff can be written as $\Pr(\theta \geq \theta_c \,|x_i, y, z)$ $-p$, which is equal to

$$\int_{\theta_c}^{\infty} \phi\left(\sqrt{\alpha+\beta+\gamma}\left(\theta - \frac{\alpha y + \beta x_i + \gamma(z-b)}{\alpha+\beta+\gamma}\right)\right) d\theta - p, \tag{3}$$

where $\phi(.)$ is the normal density function. In other words, the expected payoff equals the survival probability minus the bond price. The expression states that the payoff increases with the posterior. The payoff is also higher, the smaller the critical state θ_c. With a smaller critical state, the range of fundamentals, in which the firm repays its debt, increases, thus increasing the expected payoff.

The critical state of the fundamentals indicates the situation when the financial resources of the firm are exhausted through early foreclosure, i.e. when the mass of foreclosing investors cannot be disbursed anymore. Therefore, the critical state is called default point. The mass of foreclosing investors l are all investors receiving signals below a threshold x^* indicating states worse than θ_c. Hence, $l = \Pr(x_i < x^* \,|\theta)$, or:

$$l = \int_{-\infty}^{x^*} \phi\left(\sqrt{\beta}(x - \theta_c)\right) dx. \tag{4}$$

2.2. Uniqueness and Equilibrium

In determining the outcome of the game I follow the reasoning of Atkeson (2001). Assuming an investor gets a bad signal x_0 that indicates a fundamental state $\theta < \underline{\theta}$, foreclosure exhausts the financial reserves of the firm. Thereby it is sufficient, that only one investor forecloses. Moreover, the signal x_0 is the highest signal for which the investor knows, that, independent of the behavior of others, her payoff is negative $\Pr(\theta \geq \underline{\theta}\,|x_0) - p < 0$. Since investors are rational, she second guesses that every investor with a signal $x < x_0$ also expects a negative payoff and hence forecloses. Therefore, the fraction $\Pr(x < x_0\,|\theta)$ of investors forecloses. Knowing that in state $\underline{\theta}$, she is not the only investor who forecloses, there exists a state $\theta_0 > \underline{\theta}$ in which foreclosure is still sufficient to exhaust the financial reserves of the firm. Hence, her payoff for a signal $x_1 = x_0 + \xi$, where ξ is a small positive number, is still negative $\Pr(\theta \geq \theta_0\,|x_0) - p < 0$. Again she second guesses that all investors with signals $x < x_1$ foreclose, which are actually less than for signal x_0. This reasoning produces an increasing sequence $\langle x_n, \theta_n \rangle_{n=0}^{\infty}$.

On the other hand, if an investor gets a good signal x^0 which indicates a fundamental state $\theta \geq \overline{\theta}$, the firm is liquid. Thereby, x^0 is the lowest signal assuring a positive payoff $\Pr\left(\theta \geq \overline{\theta}\,|x^0\right) - p > 0$. Hence, she can guess that all investors with signals $x \geq x^0$ remain invested, i.e. fraction $\Pr(x \geq x^0\,|\theta)$ remains invested. Thus, there exists a $\theta^0 < \overline{\theta}$ where the remaining capital is sufficient to finance the firm. Now, knowing that financing is secured in θ^0, signal $x^1 = x^0 - \xi$ is the lowest signal assuring a positive payoff for investing $\Pr(\theta \geq \theta^0\,|x^1) - p > 0$. Continuing with this argumentation produces a decreasing sequence $\langle x^n, \theta^n \rangle_{n=0}^{\infty}$.

A unique equilibrium exists, if both sequences converge to a joint solution (x^*, θ_c). Therefore, the limit points of the sequences have to be solutions to equations (3) and (4). Hence, a unique joined solution of these equations gives the equilibrium.

I rewrite the equations (3) and (4) in terms of cumulative distribution functions (cdf) $\Phi(.)$. An investor is indifferent between rolling over and foreclosing if

$$1 - \Phi\left(\sqrt{\alpha+\beta+\gamma}\left(\theta_c - \frac{\alpha y + \beta x^* + \gamma(z-b)}{\alpha+\beta+\gamma}\right)\right) = p, \tag{5}$$

therefore condition (5) is called indifference condition.

The firm is illiquid if the mass of foreclosing investors l amounts to the critical fundamental state θ_c:

$$\Phi\left(\sqrt{\beta}\,(x^* - \theta_c)\right) = \theta_c, \tag{6}$$

therefore condition (6) is called illiquidity condition.

Solving (5) for x^* and inserting in (6) yields the equilibrium condition

$$\theta_c = \Phi\left(\frac{\alpha+\gamma}{\sqrt{\beta}}\left(\theta_c - \frac{\alpha y + \gamma(z-b)}{\alpha+\gamma} + \Phi^{-1}(p)\frac{\sqrt{\alpha+\beta+\gamma}}{\alpha+\gamma}\right)\right), \tag{7}$$

where $\Phi^{-1}(.)$ is the inverse of the standard normal cumulative distribution function.[38] The default point is thus defined through an implicit function that can be interpreted as a cumulative normal distribution with mean $\frac{\alpha y+\gamma(z+b)}{\alpha+\gamma} - \Phi^{-1}(p)\frac{\sqrt{\alpha+\beta+\gamma}}{\alpha+\gamma}$ and precision $\frac{\alpha+\gamma}{\sqrt{\beta}}$ (cf. Morris and Shin 2004).[39]

Thus, a sufficient condition for the equilibrium to be unique is, that the slope of the right hand side of (7) is smaller than 1, i.e. $\frac{\alpha+\gamma}{\sqrt{\beta}}\phi < 1$ (see appendix 5.1). Since the normal density has a maximum at $\left(0, \frac{1}{\sqrt{2\pi}}\right)$ the uniqueness condition can be written as:

$$\frac{\alpha+\gamma}{\sqrt{\beta}} < \sqrt{2\pi}. \tag{8}$$

Including the rating makes the cumulative distribution steeper. Thus, it also puts a tighter bound on the restriction of parameters that ensures unique equilibria (cf. Carlson and Hale 2006).

Figure (II.2) displays a graphical representation of equation (7). The default point is the intersection between the cumulative distribution and the 45°-line.

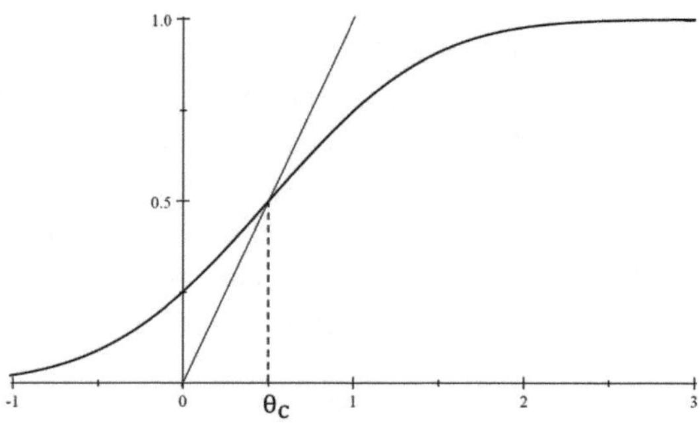

Figure II.2.: **Equilibrium condition:** The cumulative normal distribution represents the right hand side of the equilibrium equation (7) and equals the mass of foreclosing investors. The 45°-line represents the mass of investors who can be redeemed. The intersection determines the default point θ_c.

For realizations of θ bigger than θ_c the firm can pay back its debt. Since $\theta_c \in [0,1]$, the firm can always pay if $\theta > 1$ and the firm is insolvent if $\theta < 0$ (cf. Obstfeld 1996). For

[38] A derivation of (7) is given in appendix 5.1.

[39] Note that for $\gamma = 0$, i.e. the rating contains no information, the equilibrium condition (7) reduces to the no rating case as discussed in Morris and Shin (2004) and is given in appendix 5.1 equation (18).

intermediate fundamentals, $0 \leq \theta \leq 1$, the firm is always solvent but its liquidity depends on the fraction of foreclosing investors. The mass of foreclosing investors is given by the cumulative distribution, while the mass of investors who can be redeemed is given by the 45°-line. Hence, to the left of the intersection, i.e. $[0, \theta_c]$, foreclosure exceeds the financing capacity of the firm. Liquidation is therefore "inefficient" since the firm is still solvent but illiquid (cf. Morris and Shin, 2004). To the right of the intersection, i.e. $]\theta_c, 1]$ the firm is solvent and liquid.

The unique equilibrium is stable. If out of equilibrium beliefs indicate a hypothetical default point $\widehat{\theta}_c$ below the actual default point ($[0, \theta_c]$), investors expect a negative payoff and foreclose. If, however, beliefs indicate that $\widehat{\theta}_c$ is above the actual default point ($]\theta_c, 1]$), investors expect a positive payoff and roll over. Hence, in the inefficient region $\widehat{\theta}_c$ grows, while in the liquid region $\widehat{\theta}_c$ declines. This adaption leads to a stable unique equilibrium.

2.3. Comparative Statics

In this section, I turn to the question how the default point is influenced through the rating, the public information, the bond price, and the bias.

2.3.1. Rating

Introducing a rating changes the level of information of every investor and therefore changes the mean and the precision of the posterior. An improvement of the rating induces investors to conclude that the fundamental state has improved. This implies a higher survival probability and increases the expected payoff. Hence, less investors foreclose and the default point decreases. This relation is described by the default sensitivity of the rating, which is given by the derivative of the equilibrium condition (7) with respect to the rating. Through applying the implicit function theorem I get:[40]

$$\frac{\partial \theta_c}{\partial z} = -\frac{\frac{\gamma}{\sqrt{\beta}}\phi\left(.\right)}{1 - \frac{\alpha+\gamma}{\sqrt{\beta}}\phi\left(.\right)}. \tag{9}$$

Where ϕ is the standard normal density with the argument (.) given by (7). If the uniqueness condition (8) holds, i.e. $\frac{\alpha+\gamma}{\sqrt{\beta}}\phi < 1$, the denominator is always positive, so that the relation between rating and default point is negative. This relation is shown in an implicit plot in figure II.4 on page 77.

Figure (II.3) shows how the inclusion of the rating changes the equilibrium. The plot shows both sides of the equilibrium condition, the identity function and the cumulative

[40]Derivations of the default sensitivities are given in appendix 5.2.

normal distribution (cdf). For a rating with the same precision and mean as public information the cdf gets steeper (dotted line) than in the case without rating (dashed line). The even steeper solid line represents a rating with higher precision and the gray line represents a rating with an observed positive bias.

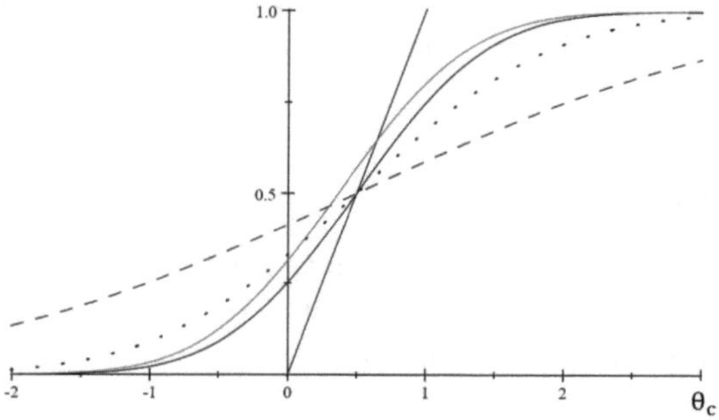

Figure II.3.: **Rating's influence on the default point:** The figure shows the implicit equilibrium condition (7) for different specifications of the rating. The dashed line represents the no rating case, the dotted line the case where the rating is equivalent to public information. The solid lines represent a higher precision of the rating, where the gray line has a positive bias and the black line is unbiased.

The distribution of the posterior (1) resembles a mapping that determines the share of investors having a certain belief about the fundamental state. Hence, a point on the posterior's curve in figure II.1 equals the share of investors holding the belief that the fundamentals are at least θ. Through including the rating in the formation of beliefs, the posterior becomes more concentrated, i.e. its variance decreases. The higher concentration of beliefs implies that more investors hold beliefs located near the posterior's mean and accordingly less investors have diverging beliefs compared to the case without a rating (cf. gray line and dashed gray line in figure II.1). Hence, more investors adapt their investment position resulting in a heightened sensitivity around the mean of the equilibrium cdf.

In figure II.3 the inclusion of the rating has no effect on the selected equilibrium.[41] In this case the default point is at 0.5 and according to (6) the share of investors foreclosing is also 0.5. These are all investors with signals $x_i < x^*$. With $y = z = 0.5$ the distribution of investors' beliefs is symmetric around 0.5 and the inclusion of the rating or any alteration in the precision does not change the equilibrium.

If the default point is below 0.5, the inclusion of an unbiased rating increases the share of investors that belief in states lower than 0.5. Hence, the rating lowers the default point further, which leads to an increase in foreclosure. However, for default points above 0.5,

[41]This only applies if the unconditional expectations of the rating and of public information both are 0.5.

an unbiased rating confirms the good perception about the fundamental state, leading to increased rollover. Hence, the default point increases. The inclusion of an unbiased rating rewards good borrowers and punishes bad borrowers. A rating agency that assesses the fundamental state of a firm must therefore take its own influence into account. When a rating is issued its coordination effect changes the default point. For a correct assessment the rating agency must therefore incorporate its own coordination effect on the behavior of speculators.

2.3.2. Public Information

For equal precision $\alpha = \gamma$, the impact of public information on the default point is identical to the impact of the rating. A change in information that indicates a better fundamental state increases the expected payoff, so that less investors foreclose and the default point decreases. Differentiating the equilibrium condition (7) with respect to y gives the default sensitivity of public information

$$\frac{\partial \theta_c}{\partial y} = -\frac{\frac{\alpha}{\sqrt{\beta}}\phi\left(.\right)}{1 - \frac{\alpha+\gamma}{\sqrt{\beta}}\phi\left(.\right)}, \tag{10}$$

which is negative, if the uniqueness condition (8) is fulfilled.

The rating also influences the processing of public information by investors. Since investors weigh every signal according to its precision the introduction of the rating increases the part of information that is shared by investors. This reduces the strategic uncertainty about the behavior of other investors and allows a better coordination. Hence, less investors foreclose for good public information, while more investors foreclose for bad public information compared to the no rating case (cf. figure II.4).

2.3.3. Bond Price

Not only changes in information alter the behavior, also a change in the price, for which a bond can be redeemed, leads to a reassessment of the investor's decision. An increase in the bond price raises the opportunity costs of investing and accordingly reduces the expected payoff of the investment. Investors having been indifferent before the bond price change, now, face a negative expected payoff and, hence, decide to foreclose. Necessarily, the default point increases with the mass of foreclosing investors. The illiquidity condition (6) states that all investors with signals below a threshold, conditional on the default point, foreclose. With the increased default point the threshold signal increases as well. In turn, the changes of x^* and θ_c induce a decline of the survival probability and an increase of

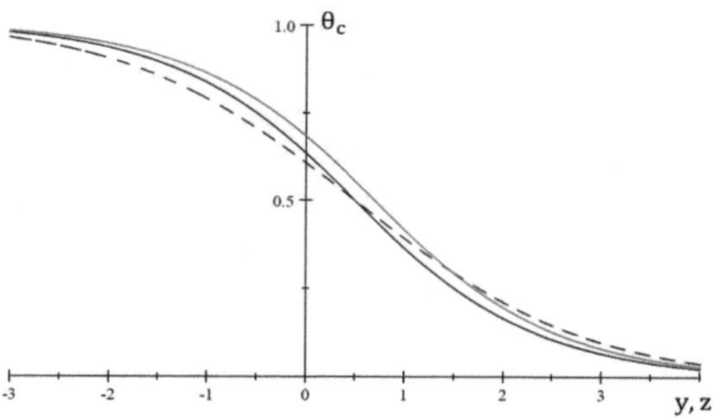

Figure II.4.: **Implicit relation of public information or rating and default point:** Plotted are the cases: no rating (dashed), rating with higher precission (solid black) and rating with positive bias (gray). Here $b = 0.2$ and $p = 0.5$. Moreover, precision is equal, i.e. $\alpha = \gamma = 1$, so that the explanatory variable can be either public information y or the rating z, where either $z = 0.5$ or $y = 0.5$.

the expected payoff till investors are again indifferent. The default sensitivity of the bond price is:

$$\frac{\partial \theta_c}{\partial p} = \frac{1}{\phi\left(\Phi^{-1}\left(p\right)\right)} \frac{\phi\left(.\right)\sqrt{1+\frac{\alpha+\gamma}{\beta}}}{1-\phi\left(.\right)\frac{\alpha+\gamma}{\sqrt{\beta}}}. \tag{11}$$

In case the uniqueness condition is fulfilled (8), i.e. $\frac{\alpha+\gamma}{\sqrt{\beta}}\phi < 1$, every factor is positive confirming that θ_c increases in p.

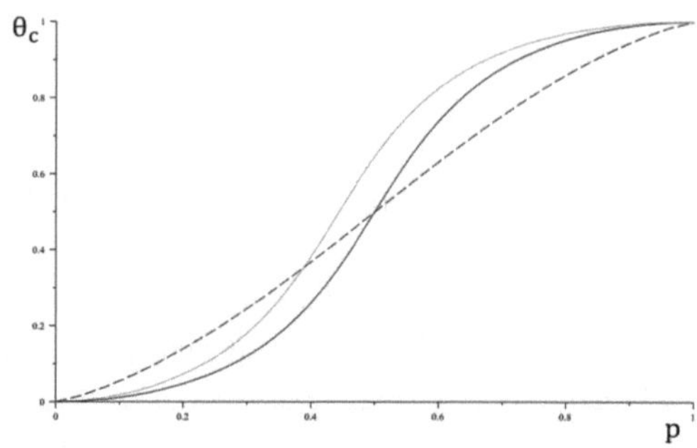

Figure II.5.: **Implicit relation of bond price and default point:** The figure shows the relationship between the bond price and the default point for the cases: no rating (dashed), rating with higher precision (black), and biased rating (gray). Here, $b = 0.2$ and $y = z = 0.5$.

Figure II.5 shows that the inclusion of the rating increases the sensitivity around the posterior mean and decreases the sensitivity at the tails (solid black line).

Compared to public information and the rating, the bond price differs in that it is bounded on the interval $[0, 1]$. If the bond price equals 0, there are no opportunity costs of rolling over and the expected payoff is always greater or equal zero $\Pr(\theta \geq \theta_c) - 0 \geq 0$. In this case, all investors roll over and the default point becomes 0, implying a survival probability of 1. On the other hand, if the bond price is 1, the expected payoff is always lower or equal to zero $\Pr(\theta \geq \theta_c) - 1 \leq 0$. Hence, all investors foreclose and the default point becomes 1 implying a default probability of 1.

2.3.4. Bias

He et al. (2011) and Griffin and Tang (2011) find that some rating agencies were too generous in distributing their initial ratings before the crisis. As reasons, high complexity of products, increasing competition, reputation, and incentives are named (cf. e.g. Skreta and Veldkamp 2009 and Bolton et al. 2012). Therefore, I show how an observable bias influences the coordination of investors and the equilibrium.

The bias is a systematic part of the error term and is common knowledge. During the assessment process investors correct their posterior beliefs for this systematic error. If a rating with a positive bias is observed, investors know that the actual fundamental state is worse than the projected. Therefore, they lower their beliefs accordingly. As stated before, the revised or conditional fundamental state is $\theta | z \sim N\left(z - b, \frac{1}{\gamma}\right)$. Hence, investors reduce their expectations about the true fundamental state. Consequently, their expected payoffs decline resulting in a higher foreclosure rate and a higher default point (cf. figure II.3).

The bias also influences the impact of public information and the bond price on the default point.

An observed bias reduces the posterior belief for any given public information received. Hence, with a bias more investors foreclose and the default point increases for any given public signal (gray line in figure II.4).

The bias, if observed and positive, reduces the posterior and hence reduces the expected payoff. For a given bond price the expected payoff becomes negative, so that more investors foreclose and the default point increases (gray line in figure II.5).

In case of an increase of the bias, the posterior belief about the fundamental state is reduced. Contrary to the rating change, the increased bias reduces the survival probability implying a negative payoff of rolling over. Investors will decide to foreclose and thereby raise the default point. The default sensitivity of the bias is

$$\frac{\partial \theta_c}{\partial b} = \frac{\frac{\gamma}{\sqrt{\beta}}\phi\left(.\right)}{1 - \frac{\alpha+\gamma}{\sqrt{\beta}}\phi\left(.\right)}, \tag{12}$$

which, under the uniqueness condition (8), is apparently positive. The foreclosure rate increases over the complete fundamentals space and bad borrowers as well as good borrowers are punished.

Investors process information to assess the fundamental state. Every signal allows the update of the conditional expectation about the true state. The question remains what fundamental state the rating implies compared to public information. Comparing the conditional expectations of the rating and of public information, the expected state after observing the rating can be higher, equal, or lower, depending on the stochastic error, i.e. the precision. For a lower rating, i.e. $z - b < y$, a lower state is implied by the rating. The mean of the equilibrium cdf shifts to the left and the default point increases. The opposite happens for a higher rating, i.e. $z - b > y$, then the mean of the equilibrium cdf shifts to the right and the default point decreases. For equal signals i.e. $z - b = y$, the rating strengthens the beliefs of investors resulting either in an increase or a decrease in the default point depending on the fundamental state.[42]

2.4. Transparency and Multiple Equilibria

Having considered the impact of changes in information, bias, and bond price, I turn to the question, how a change in the precision of information alters the default point. For simplicity I only consider the case $p = 0.5$ so that the inverse cumulative equals zero, i.e. $\Phi^{-1}\left(0.5\right) = 0$. Then, the public information posterior $\frac{\alpha y+\gamma(z-b)}{\alpha+\gamma}$ is equal to the mean of the equilibrium cdf.[43]

If the precision of signals increases, investors' beliefs become more concentrated. Put differently, the fraction of investors holding beliefs near the mean of the posterior increases. For a bad public information posterior, i.e. $\theta|\, y, z \in [0, 0.5[$, increasing the precision of public information increases the fraction of investors who belief in bad states. Hence, foreclosure rises and the default point increases (cf. (13) and panel a of figure II.6).

In case of a good public information posterior, i.e. $\theta|\, y, z \in]0.5, 1]$, increasing public information precision makes more investors belief in good states. Consequently, they roll over and the default point decreases (cf. (13) and panel b of figure II.6).

[42]The exception $z - b = y = 0.5$ is discussed in the rating section 2.3.1.

[43]For $p \neq 0.5$, changes in the precision influence the expected payoff and hence the default point. The influence of the bond price is discussed in section 2.3.3 in detail.

If instead, the private information precision increases, the belief formation is different. For bad public posteriors, it is more likely to get a private signal that indicates a better state than one indicating a state worse. Now, if the precision of this private signal increases, investors put more weight on their private information, which on average indicates a better state than the public posterior. Consequently, the common posterior increases, more investors roll over and the default point decreases (cf. (14) and panel a of figure II.7).

For good information public posteriors, however, it is more likely to get a bad private signal. Hence, the common posterior decreases with private precision rising. More investors foreclose and the default point increases (cf. (14) and panel b of figure II.7).

Here, I consider an unbiased rating, i.e. the unconditional expectations of public information and the rating are equal $y = z$. Without a rating the weight investors put on this unconditional expectation in their posterior is reduced. Consequently, for a given precision less investors foreclose in bad states and more foreclose in good states. This relation is shown by the dashed line in figure II.6. The same holds when considering private information precision, cf. figure II.7.

Multiple Equilibria For low private information precision, signals are widely dispersed and point to good as well as bad states. If public information precision is high, investors can coordinate on low as well as on high default points, which give the same survival probability and, hence, the same expected payoff for different posteriors. Since, this is a matter of weighing information, the absolute precision is irrelevant. What counts, is the relative precision of public and private information. Multiple equilibria emerge if public information is precise relative to private information.

The sensitivity of the default point θ_c with respect to the precision of public information α is:[44]

$$\frac{\partial \theta_c}{\partial \alpha} = \phi\left(.\right) \frac{2\sqrt{\alpha+\beta+\gamma}\left(\theta_c - y\right) + \Phi^{-1}\left(p\right)}{2\sqrt{\beta}\sqrt{\alpha+\beta+\gamma}\left(1 - \frac{\alpha+\gamma}{\sqrt{\beta}}\phi\left(.\right)\right)} \tag{13}$$

If the uniqueness condition (8) holds, the denominator is always positive. The numerator is positive if $\theta_c > y - \frac{\Phi^{-1}(p)}{2\sqrt{\alpha+\beta+\gamma}}$ and negative otherwise. In bad states (panel a of figure II.6), the numerator is positive implying a positive relation between public information precision and the default point. In good states (panel b), the relation is negative. When the uniqueness condition is violated the denominator changes its sign. Then the additional values of θ_c imply an increasing relation and simultaneously a decreasing relation of the

[44]Derivations of the sensitivities are given in appendix 5.3. The sensitivity of the default point with respect to the rating is also given in the appendix. Since the structure is not different from the public information sensitivity, the rating is omitted in the text.

precision and the default point. The implicit relations are shown in figure II.6.[45]

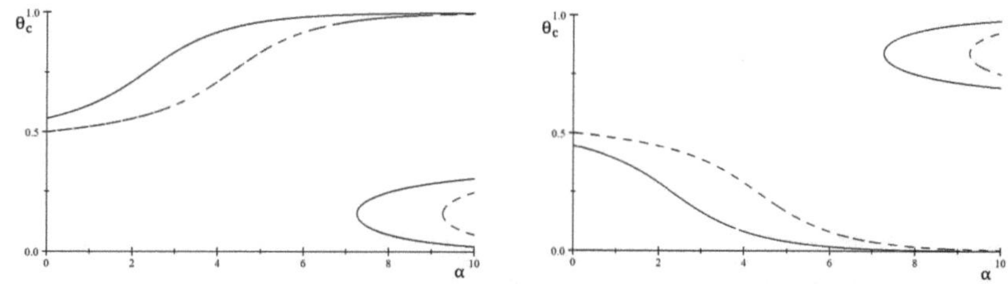

(a) $y = z = 0.4$ (b) $y = z = 0.6$

Figure II.6.: **Implicit relation of public information precision and default point for varying unconditional expectations:** With (solid) and without rating (dashed).

The gap between multiple equilibria just depends on the mean of the equilibrium distribution. For infinite public information precision the equilibrium cdf jumps from 0 to 1 at exactly its mean. Therefore, the middle equilibrium equals the public information posterior. In this case investors share the same posterior beliefs about the state of the economy. In other words, the posterior is common knowledge. Consequently, all investors either foreclose or roll over.[46] Thereby the investors' expectations about the fundamental state loose their effect on determining the outcome—only coordination matters.

With imprecise public signals, i.e. precision equals zero, the equilibrium cdf becomes uninformative, disclosing no information about the underlying state.[47]

The sensitivity of the default point θ_c with respect to the precision of private information β is:

$$\frac{\partial \theta_c}{\partial \beta} = \phi(.) \frac{\alpha(y-\theta_c) + \gamma(z-b-\theta_c) - \Phi^{-1}(p)\frac{\alpha+\gamma}{\sqrt{\alpha+\beta+\gamma}}}{2\beta^{\frac{3}{2}}\left(1-\phi(.)\frac{\alpha+\gamma}{\sqrt{\beta}}\right)}. \tag{14}$$

The numerator is positive if $\theta_c < \frac{\alpha y+\gamma(z-b)}{\alpha+\gamma} - \Phi^{-1}(p)\frac{1}{\sqrt{\alpha+\beta+\gamma}}$ and negative otherwise. For relatively low private information precision, the uniqueness condition is violated and multiple equilibria obtain that vanish with increasing precision. The relation between private information precision and the default point is positive for good states and negative for bad states. The relations are shown in figure II.7.

[45]A graphical interpretation and plots showing the emergence of multiple equilibria are given in appendix 5.3.

[46]In regions where a liquidation is inefficient, i.e. the equilibrium cdf is above the 45°-line, the foreclosure rate increases (cf. section 2.2). On the contrary, in regions where the firm is liquid, i.e. the equilibrium cdf is below the 45°-line, the foreclosure rate declines. Consequently, only the upper and lower equilibrium are stable, while the middle equilibrium is unstable.

[47]This holds only for $\alpha \wedge \gamma \to 0$.

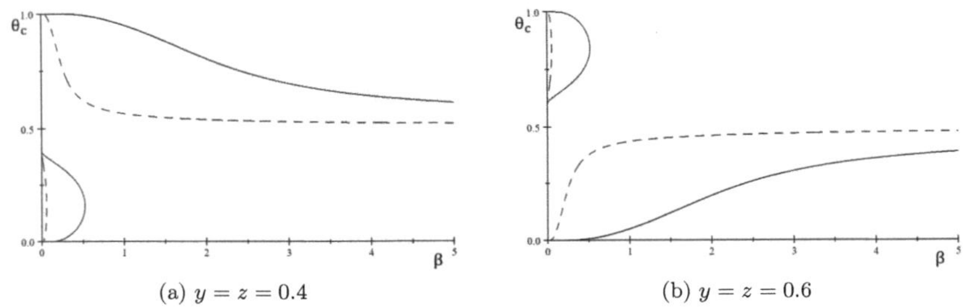

Figure II.7.: **Implicit relation of private information precision and default point for varying unconditional expectations:** With (solid) and without rating (dashed).

If the precision of private information gets infinite, each investor's posterior equals her private signal x_i. This is when beliefs are most dispersed. Consequently, coordination is not possible and the equilibrium is unique.

For imprecise private signals, investors again share the same posterior beliefs enabling perfect coordination, so that multiple equilibria emerge.

3. Pricing Bonds

What is the price investors should expect for a bond of the firm? The price for which an investor is willing to sell her bond depends on the payoff she expects from holding the bond. As stated before, a bond pays 1 in case the firm survives and 0 if it fails. Hence, the expected payoff equals the survival probability. If the bond price is above the expected payoff, investors take the profit and foreclose. For bond prices below, investors roll over, so that in equilibrium the survival probability equals the bond price and investors are indifferent between foreclosure and rollover.

To show the effect of the rating on the pricing of debt, I first present a bond price based on public information with and without the coordination effect as in Morris and Shin (2004). Then I show how the inclusion of the rating alters the pricing method.[48]

Morris and Shin propose a naive pricing method, which applies for a single investor in the market, who is not affected by strategic uncertainty. The single investor must not worry about the beliefs of others. The investor only considers the underlying state based on public information and derives the following price

$$P_{naive} = \int_{0}^{\infty} \phi\left(\sqrt{\alpha}\left(\theta - y\right)\right) d\theta = \Phi\left(\sqrt{\alpha} y\right). \tag{15}$$

The naive price P_{naive} is the probability that the realization of the fundamentals is greater than zero, $\theta > 0$. Then, for a single investor, the firm is solvent and liquid.

Morris and Shin argue that this pricing method neglects the influence of coordination on the default point of the firm. When the fundamental state deteriorates the default probability rises, more investors foreclose and the default point increases. For providing their capital to a firm that has become riskier investors demand a discount. The price proposed by Morris and Shin P_{ms} equals the survival probability based on public information

$$P_{ms} = \int_{\theta_c}^{\infty} \phi\left(\sqrt{\alpha}\left(\theta - y\right)\right) d\theta = \Phi\left(\sqrt{\alpha}\left(y - \theta_c\right)\right). \tag{16}$$

The compensation for the increased risk through the possible coordination is simply the default point. Since the default point is an implicit function of public information $\theta_c(y)$

[48]The proposed pricing methods differ from the bond price considered before in that they do not include private information.

the compensation increases when the fundamental state deteriorates, c.f. (10). With the default point being greater or equal zero the Morris and Shin price is always lower or equal the naive price. Neglecting the coordination effect leads to an overpricing of debt through the naive pricing method that increases with a declining public signal. Figure II.8 shows the evolution of the prices as a function of the unconditional expectation.

Including the rating increases the default sensitivity of the fundamentals which allows an even better coordination between investors that further alters the bond price. Again the bond price equals the survival probability. Since private information is not considered, I call the price conditional on public information and the rating, forecasted price:[49]

$$\begin{aligned} P(y,z,b) &= \int_{\theta_c}^{\infty} \phi\left(\sqrt{\alpha+\gamma}\left(\theta - \frac{\alpha y + \gamma(z-b)}{\alpha+\gamma}\right)\right) d\theta \\ &= \Phi\left(\sqrt{\alpha+\gamma}\left(\frac{\alpha y + \gamma(z-b)}{\alpha+\gamma} - \theta_c\right)\right). \end{aligned} \tag{17}$$

Note that the default point is now an implicit function of public information and the rating $\theta_c(y,z)$. With the rating the bond price adapts more rapidly to changes in fundamentals. As before the rating concentrates beliefs about the underlying state around the public information posterior $\frac{\alpha y+\gamma(z-b)}{\alpha+\gamma}$. The higher concentration of beliefs appears in the higher slope of the cdf $\sqrt{\alpha+\gamma}$, which accounts for the lower variance of the posterior. The increased precision in the assessment of the fundamental state reveals that only bad states are overpriced by the naive method, while good states are underpriced. The same holds for the Morris and Shin pricing method: it underprices good states and overprices bad states. Including the rating increases the bond price of good borrowers and decreases the bond price of bad borrowers. Put differently, good borrowers pay a lower yield, while bad borrowers have to pay a higher compensation for the risk. The inclusion of the rating allows for a more effective pricing since expectations about the underlying fundamentals have a lower variance which leads to a greater consensus about the expected survival probability and hence the bond price.

To derive the prices I calculate two types of default points θ_c. One from the equilibrium condition omitting the rating $\theta_c(y)$ (18), the other from the equilibrium condition including the rating $\theta_c(y,z)$ (7). Therefor I use a sequence of y, z, where I assume that $y = z$ and $b = 0$. As result I obtain pairs (y, θ_c) and (y, z, θ_c) solving the equilibrium conditions. Through inserting these pairs in the pricing equations (16) and (17), I get the Morris and Shin price P_{ms} as well as the forecasted price P. The results are shown in figure II.8.[50] Note that the prices are conditional on θ_c, so that multiple equilibria do

[49]In this sense, the Morris and Shin price and the naive price are also price forecasts.

[50]The naive price P_{naive} is simply a normal distribution with mean 0 and standard deviation $\frac{1}{\sqrt{\alpha}}$.

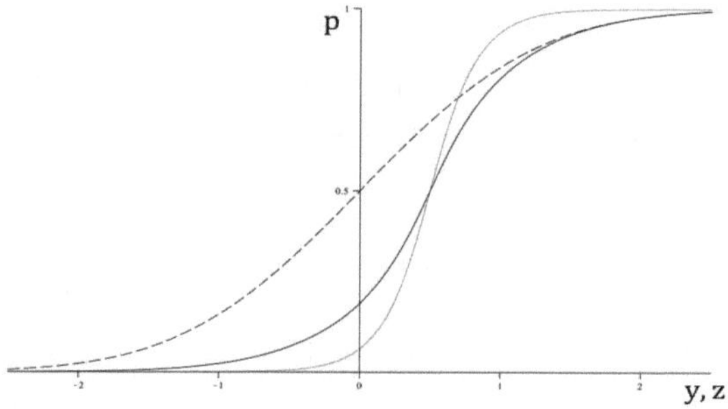

Figure II.8.: **Pricing methods:** Plotted are the naive price (dashed), the Morris and Shin price (black) and the forecasted price (gray).

not exist in the prices themselves.

An observed positive bias reduces the posterior expectation of the investors and results in a higher foreclosure rate. Consequently, the bond price is lower for any given public signal, i.e. the price curve would shift to the right. This shift is bigger the higher the bias is.

Deviations of the rating z from public information y can result from the fact that ratings are not updated continuously. Hence, a company that is improving its fundamental state exhibits a lower posterior belief till the rating is updated. This leads to a significant risk premium that is only due to the information lag and not to underlying risk. Therefore, daily assessments of risk through Merton type models as the Moody's KMV, that use option pricing strategies to derive a probability of default, prevent from big disparities that can emerge between rating updates.

Morris and Shin (2004) show that the overpricing through the naive price increases with public information deteriorating (cf. black line in figure II.9 and column $\frac{P_{naive}}{P_{MS}}$ in table 3.1). This increasing effect of the default point is also reflected in the default sensitivities of the rating and of public information, cf. (9) and (10). The sensitivities show that the default point increases with deteriorating signals.

Table 3.1 compares the overpricing of the different pricing methods. The first column gives the unconditional expectation of public information and the rating. The second row gives the overpricing for an expected fundamental state of 0. Thereby, the naive price is 2.65 times higher than the Morris and Shin price and 7.89 times higher than the forecasted price, while the Morris and Shin price is 2.98 times higher than the forecasted price. For an expected fundamental state of 0.5 P_{MS} and P are equal, while for an unconditional expectation of 1 P_{MS} is only 0.87 times P and P_{naive} is only 0.90 times P. For even better

y, z	$\frac{P_{naive}}{P_{MS}}$	$\frac{P_{naive}}{P}$	$\frac{P_{MS}}{P}$
−0.5	4.42	13.2	58.4
0	2.65	7.89	2.98
0.5	1.38	1.38	1.00
1	1.04	0.90	0.87
2	1.00	0.98	0.98

Table 3.1.: Unconditional expectations and relative prices

fundamental states the bond prices converge to 1 and the underpricing vanishes. On the contrary, for bad fundamental states bond prices converge to 0 and overpricing increases superlinearly (cf. figure II.9).

Omitting the rating in the pricing of debt neglects additional information and the effect on the concentration of beliefs. This coordination effect leads to more investors foreclosing in bad states as well as more investors rolling over in good states. Hence, the survival probability and with it the expected payoff of the investment increase in good states and decrease in bad states. With a higher expected payoff in good states investors demand a higher bond price at which they agree to foreclose. Contrary, in a bad state where the expected payoff is low investors agree to foreclose at lower bond prices. Consequently, the bond prices increase in good states and decrease in bad states. Including the rating shows that the Morris and Shin pricing method underprices good debt and an overprices bad debt.

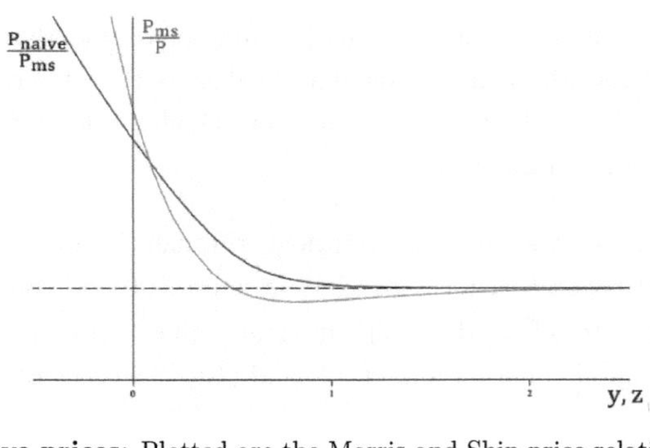

Figure II.9.: **Relative prices:** Plotted are the Morris and Shin price relative to the naive price (black) and the forecasted price relative to the Morris and Shin price (gray). Above the horizontal line the benchmark method overprices debt below the benchmark method underprices debt.

The dashed line in figure II.9 shows, where the bond prices of the three methods are identical. Above the dashed line the benchmark prices (numerator) are higher below the benchmark prices are lower. The black line shows that, compared to Morris and Shin, the naive method results in higher bond prices over the complete fundamentals space. The overpricing grows superlinearly in bad states, while in good states bond prices converge. Thus, bad borrowers are rewarded by inadvertent discounts, while with increasing solvency the discount vanishes. The gray line shows that, compared to the forecasted price, the Morris and Shin method overprices bad borrowers and underprices good borrowers. The negligence of the rating rewards bad borrowers and punishes good borrowers.

The rating has a significant influence on the bond price and hence the yield of bonds. When the rating is intended to give an investment advise its own influence on the behavior of investors has to be taken into account. Especially for bad borrowers the rating has a huge influence on the bond price and thus the refinancing capability of the borrowers. Neglecting the rating in the pricing misjudges the bond price severely.

The empirical literature extensively analyzes the effect of rating changes on stock prices. Thereby, it confirms that the rating's impact is especially important for bad borrowers. Dichev and Piotroski (2001) find that stock prices of bad borrowers react strongly to rating downgrades. Jorion and Zhang (2007) add that upgrades are important for bad borrowers. Also these studies focus on stock prices, they show that publicly available information has a stronger effect on bad than on good borrowers.

4. Conclusion

I reviewed an investor coordination game, as analyzed in Morris and Shin (2004), and added a biased rating. When observing a positive bias, investors know that the signal is sugarcoated and that the underlying state is actually worse. Hence, investors adjust their beliefs by subtracting the bias. With lower conditional expectations more investors foreclose raising the default point.

The bond price influences the expected payoff. An increase in the bond price reduces the payoff and makes foreclosing more profitable. Hence, the foreclosure rate and the default point increase.

When considering the impact of a rating on the pricing of debt, neglecting the rating leads to an overpricing of bad borrowers and an underpricing of good borrowers. Omitting the rating, in good states, decreases the conditional expectations of investors. The negligence causes a higher foreclosure rate at the cost of the good firm, which has to compensate for the higher perceived risk through a higher yield. However, in bad states ignoring the rating increases the conditional expectations of investors. Resulting in a lower foreclosure rate, benefiting the bad borrower, who pays a lower yield.

Firms evolve continuously with the consequence that a divergence emerges between the rating and the underlying fundamental state. When the firm evolves positively the rating still indicates a lower fundamental state. As a consequence more investors foreclose compared to a situation where the rating is adapted. On the other hand, when the fundamental state of the firm deteriorates the rating still indicates a higher fundamental state and less investors foreclose. This time lag between rating updates distorts the posterior expectations. It thereby benefits firms with deteriorating fundamentals and punishes firms with improving fundamentals. In addition to the rating, market based risk models, that allow daily assessments of risk, can prevent from big disparities that can emerge between rating updates.

A rating claims to assess the credit quality of a firm. Since the issuance coordinates investors' beliefs and alters their behavior, the rating agency must take its own influence into account. Neglecting the endogeneity of the rating necessarily leads to a wrong assessment. Especially for bad borrowers the coordination effect and, hence, the rating's influence on the default probability and the bond price plays a major role.

5. Appendix

5.1. Equilibrium Condition and Uniqueness

To determine the equilibrium I solve the indifference condition (5) for x^*

$$x^* = -\frac{\alpha y + \gamma (z-b)}{\beta} + \Phi^{-1}(p)\frac{\sqrt{\alpha+\beta+\gamma}}{\beta} + \theta_c \frac{(\alpha+\beta+\gamma)}{\beta},$$

where I used the symmetry property of the normal distribution: $\Phi^{-1}(1-p) = -\Phi^{-1}(p)$. Inserting in the illiquidity condition (6)

$$1 - \Phi\left(\sqrt{\alpha+\beta+\gamma}\left(\theta_c - \frac{-\gamma(z-b) + \Phi^{-1}(p)\sqrt{\alpha+\beta+\gamma} + \theta_c(\alpha+\beta+\gamma) + \gamma(z-b)}{\alpha+\beta+\gamma}\right)\right) = p,$$

and rearranging gives:

$$\theta_c = \Phi\left(\frac{\alpha+\gamma}{\sqrt{\beta}}\left(\theta_c - \frac{\alpha y + \gamma(z-b)}{\alpha+\gamma} + \Phi^{-1}(p)\frac{\sqrt{\alpha+\beta+\gamma}}{\alpha+\gamma}\right)\right). \tag{7}$$

Uniqueness requires that the slope of the right hand side of the equilibrium equation (7) in the direction of θ_c is higher than the slope of the bisector on the left hand side

$$\frac{\partial\theta_c}{\partial\theta_c} > \phi(.)\frac{\alpha+\gamma}{\sqrt{\beta}} \leftrightarrow 1 > \phi(.)\frac{\alpha+\gamma}{\sqrt{\beta}} \leftrightarrow \frac{1}{\phi(.)} > \frac{\alpha+\gamma}{\sqrt{\beta}}.$$

Where $\phi(.)$ is the normal density.

For $\gamma = 0$ the equilibrium condition reduces to the no rating case given in Morris and Shin (2004):

$$\theta_c = \Phi\left(\frac{\alpha}{\sqrt{\beta}}\left(\theta_c - y + \Phi^{-1}(p)\frac{\sqrt{\alpha+\beta}}{\alpha}\right)\right). \tag{18}$$

5.2. Comparative Statics

Here, I show the derivations of the partial implicit derivatives of the equilibrium condition (7). The derivative with respect to the rating z is

$$\frac{\partial \theta_c}{\partial z} = \phi(.)\left(\frac{\alpha+\gamma}{\sqrt{\beta}}\left(\frac{\partial \theta_c}{\partial z} - \frac{\gamma}{\alpha+\gamma}\right)\right)$$

$$\frac{\partial \theta_c}{\partial z} = -\frac{\phi(.)\frac{\gamma}{\sqrt{\beta}}}{1-\phi(.)\frac{\alpha+\gamma}{\sqrt{\beta}}}. \tag{9}$$

The derivative with respect to public information y is

$$\frac{\partial \theta_c}{\partial y} = \phi(.)\left(\frac{\alpha+\gamma}{\sqrt{\beta}}\left(\frac{\partial \theta_c}{\partial y} - \frac{\alpha}{\alpha+\gamma}\right)\right)$$

$$\frac{\partial \theta_c}{\partial y} = -\frac{\phi(.)\frac{\alpha}{\sqrt{\beta}}}{1-\phi(.)\frac{\alpha+\gamma}{\sqrt{\beta}}}. \tag{10}$$

The derivative with respect to the bond price p is

$$\frac{\partial \theta_c}{\partial p} = \phi(.)\left(\frac{\alpha+\gamma}{\sqrt{\beta}}\left(\frac{\partial \theta_c}{\partial p} + \frac{\sqrt{\alpha+\beta+\gamma}}{\alpha+\gamma}\frac{1}{\phi\left(\Phi^{-1}(p)\right)}\right)\right).$$

Note that the derivative of the inverse cdf is $\Phi^{-1\prime}(p) = \frac{1}{\phi(\Phi^{-1}(p))}$, hence:

$$\frac{\partial \theta_c}{\partial p} = \frac{1}{\phi\left(\Phi^{-1}(p)\right)}\frac{\phi(.)\frac{\sqrt{\alpha+\beta+\gamma}}{\sqrt{\beta}}}{\left(1-\phi(.)\frac{\alpha+\gamma}{\sqrt{\beta}}\right)}. \tag{11}$$

The derivative with respect to the bias b is

$$\frac{\partial \theta_c}{\partial b} = \phi(.)\left(\frac{\alpha+\gamma}{\sqrt{\beta}}\left(\frac{\partial \theta_c}{\partial b} + \frac{\gamma}{\alpha+\gamma}\right)\right)$$

$$\frac{\partial \theta_c}{\partial b} = \frac{\phi(.)\frac{\gamma}{\sqrt{\beta}}}{1-\phi(.)\frac{\alpha+\gamma}{\sqrt{\beta}}}. \tag{12}$$

5.3. Transparency and Multiple Equilibria

Partial Derivatives

First I rearrange the equilibrium condition (7)

$$\theta_c = \Phi\left(\frac{\alpha+\gamma}{\sqrt{\beta}}\theta_c - \frac{\alpha y+\gamma(z-b)}{\sqrt{\beta}} + \Phi^{-1}(p)\frac{\sqrt{\alpha+\beta+\gamma}}{\sqrt{\beta}}\right).$$

Differentiating with respect to the public information precision α gives

$$\frac{\partial\theta_c}{\partial\alpha} = \phi(.)\left(\frac{1}{\sqrt{\beta}}\theta_c + \frac{\alpha+\gamma}{\sqrt{\beta}}\frac{\partial\theta_c}{\partial\alpha} - \frac{y}{\sqrt{\beta}} + \Phi^{-1}(p)\frac{1}{2\sqrt{\alpha+\beta+\gamma}\sqrt{\beta}}\right)$$

$$\frac{\partial\theta_c}{\partial\alpha} = \frac{\phi(.)(\theta_c-y)}{\sqrt{\beta}\left(1-\frac{\alpha+\gamma}{\sqrt{\beta}}\phi(.)\right)} + \frac{\phi(.)\Phi^{-1}(p)}{2\sqrt{\beta}\sqrt{\alpha+\beta+\gamma}\left(1-\frac{\alpha+\gamma}{\sqrt{\beta}}\phi(.)\right)}.$$

For the purpose of easier interpretation I build the common denominator

$$\frac{\partial\theta_c}{\partial\alpha} = \frac{\phi(.)\left(2\sqrt{\alpha+\beta+\gamma}(\theta_c-y)+\Phi^{-1}(p)\right)}{2\sqrt{\beta}\sqrt{\alpha+\beta+\gamma}\left(1-\frac{\alpha+\gamma}{\sqrt{\beta}}\phi(.)\right)}. \tag{13}$$

The derivative with respect to the precision of the rating γ is

$$\frac{\partial\theta_c}{\partial\gamma} = \phi(.)\left(\frac{1}{\sqrt{\beta}}\theta_c + \frac{\alpha+\gamma}{\sqrt{\beta}}\frac{\partial\theta_c}{\partial\gamma} - \frac{z-b}{\sqrt{\beta}} + \Phi^{-1}(p)\frac{1}{2\sqrt{\alpha+\beta+\gamma}\sqrt{\beta}}\right).$$

Rearranging

$$\frac{\partial\theta_c}{\partial\gamma} = \frac{\phi(.)(\theta_c-z+b)}{\sqrt{\beta}\left(1-\frac{\alpha+\gamma}{\sqrt{\beta}}\phi(.)\right)} + \frac{\phi(.)\Phi^{-1}(p)}{2\sqrt{\beta}\sqrt{\alpha+\beta+\gamma}\left(1-\frac{\alpha+\gamma}{\sqrt{\beta}}\phi(.)\right)}$$

gives

$$\frac{\partial\theta_c}{\partial\gamma} = \frac{\phi(.)\left(2\sqrt{\alpha+\beta+\gamma}(\theta_c-z+b)+\Phi^{-1}(p)\right)}{2\sqrt{\beta}\sqrt{\alpha+\beta+\gamma}\left(1-\frac{\alpha+\gamma}{\sqrt{\beta}}\phi(.)\right)}.$$

The derivative with respect to the private information precision β is

$$\frac{\partial\theta_c}{\partial\beta} = \phi(.)\left(-\frac{(\alpha+\gamma)\frac{1}{2}\frac{1}{\sqrt{\beta}}}{\beta}\theta_c + \frac{\alpha+\gamma}{\sqrt{\beta}}\frac{\partial\theta_c}{\partial\beta} + \frac{(\alpha y+\gamma(z-b))\frac{1}{2}\frac{1}{\sqrt{\beta}}}{\beta}\right.$$
$$\left.+\Phi^{-1}(p)\frac{\sqrt{\beta}\frac{1}{2}\frac{1}{\sqrt{\alpha+\beta+\gamma}} - \sqrt{\alpha+\beta+\gamma}\frac{1}{2}\frac{1}{\sqrt{\beta}}}{\beta}\right).$$

Rearranging

$$\frac{\partial \theta_c}{\partial \beta} - \phi(.)\frac{\alpha+\gamma}{\sqrt{\beta}}\frac{\partial \theta_c}{\partial \beta} = -\phi(.)\frac{\alpha+\gamma}{2\beta^{\frac{3}{2}}}\theta_c + \phi(.)\frac{\alpha y + \gamma(z-b)}{2\beta^{\frac{3}{2}}} + \phi(.)\,\Phi^{-1}(p)\frac{\sqrt{\beta}\frac{1}{\sqrt{\alpha+\beta+\gamma}} - \sqrt{\alpha+\beta+\gamma}\frac{1}{\sqrt{\beta}}}{2\beta}$$

$$\frac{\partial \theta_c}{\partial \beta}\left(1-\phi(.)\frac{\alpha+\gamma}{\sqrt{\beta}}\right) = -\phi(.)\frac{\alpha+\gamma}{2\beta^{\frac{3}{2}}}\theta_c + \phi(.)\frac{\alpha y + \gamma(z-b)}{2\beta^{\frac{3}{2}}} + \phi(.)\,\Phi^{-1}(p)\frac{-\frac{\alpha+\gamma}{\sqrt{\beta}\sqrt{\alpha+\beta+\gamma}}}{2\beta}$$

gives

$$\frac{\partial \theta_c}{\partial \beta} = \phi(.)\frac{\alpha(y-\theta_c) + \gamma(z-b-\theta_c) - \Phi^{-1}(p)\frac{\alpha+\gamma}{\sqrt{\alpha+\beta+\gamma}}}{2\beta^{\frac{3}{2}}\left(1-\phi(.)\frac{\alpha+\gamma}{\sqrt{\beta}}\right)}. \tag{14}$$

Emergence of multiple equilibria

Figure II.10 shows the emergence of multiple equilibria for the equilibrium cdf (7) in panel (a) and for the denominator of the sensitivity in panel (b). With increasing precision of public information the slope of the cumulative distribution (dotted) increases so that its lower bulk first tangents the 45° line (dashed) and then with even higher slope intersects the 45° line in two more points (solid). Simultaneously the denominator $1-\frac{\alpha+\gamma}{\sqrt{\beta}}\phi(.)$ becomes negative for certain values of the default point.

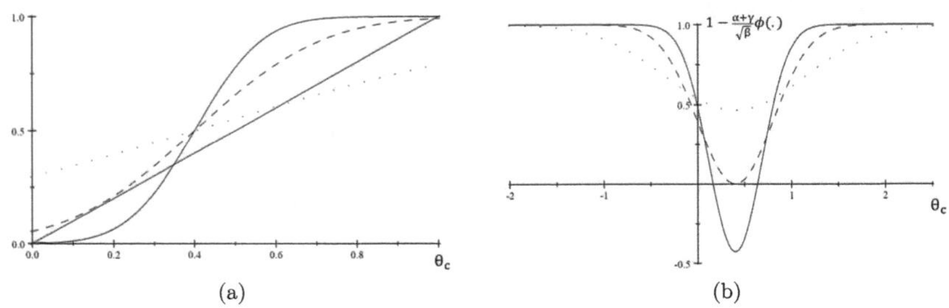

(a) (b)

Figure II.10.: **Emergence of multiple equilibria**

Part III.

Probability of Default and Precision of Information

1. Introduction

To take an investment decision, creditors can resort to a variety of information providing services like: analyst recommendations, ratings agencies, competitor analysis, investor relations services, or news agencies. How do creditors process this information, so they can build beliefs about the state of a firm, on which they base their investment decision?

In a global game, creditors receive signals about the underlying state, which are weighed according to their precision to form posterior beliefs. Upon these beliefs creditors form payoff expectations and take their investment decision.

In this paper, I present a heuristic approach that allows to compute the precision of private and public information. Thus, I show how the weight investors put on different sources of information evolves over time. To compute the precision I use forecasted and implied default probabilities in order to determine prices for standardized bonds. A standardized bond offers a repayment of 1 in case of success and a repayment of 0 in case of failure. Public and private information in the global game imply different prices. I use these prices in analogy to the standardized bond prices to obtain the weight (precision) investors put on different sources of information.

I first present a coordination game as in Morris and Shin (2004) and specify the price forecast as well as the market price implied by the coordination game. The price forecast is based on public information, while the market price is based on public and private information. A Merton KMV approach is used to forecast the survival probability that is discounted to yield the price forecast. CDS spreads determine the survival probability implied by the market, which is discounted to yield the market price. Relating the prices from the coordination game to the prices from the Merton and CDS models allows to compute the precision of public and private information.

I find that private information precision receives a higher weight in the formation of beliefs when the market default probability exceeds the forecasted default probability. Then beliefs are more dispersed and multiple equilibria are less likely. However, if the forecasted default probability exceeds the market default probability, then public information precision is weighed more. Consequently, beliefs are more concentrated and multiple equilibria are more likely.

Literature Morris and Shin (2004) analyze a standard debt contract, where investors have private information. They show that an equilibrium is unique if private information is sufficiently precise compared to public information. However, Atkeson (2001) argues that asset prices aggregate private information. The prices, being observable, serve as an additional public signal that enables investors to coordinate beliefs. Angeletos and Werning (2006) add such an asset price to the model of Morris and Shin. The asset price aggregates private information and serves as a public signal. They find that the precision of public information increases with the precision of private information. Hence, whether the equilibrium is unique depends on the aggregation.

With the advent of the standard global game literature scholars focused on the relation of public and private information and the policy aspects of disclosing information. Morris and Shin (2002) analyze the welfare effects of private and public information in a beauty contest style game, where welfare decreases with the heterogeneity of decisions. When private information is available, public information has no distinct effect on welfare and allows agents to coordinate. Hence, public information is overweighed and possible noise is magnified. Svensson (2006) comments that a higher precision of public information increases social welfare.

Bannier and Heinemann (2005) present a repeated global game of currency crises where the central bank can determine the variance in public information as well as the variance in private information. In the authors' view speculators perceive public statements as private information. In such a setting the authors suggest that countries with a low probability of crisis should minimize the variance in public information, while the variance of private information should be kept high. However, a high variance in public information accompanied with a low variance in private information is preferable for countries with a high probability of crisis.

In experiments Heinemann (2002) confirms the coordination effect of public information and finds that it reduces the threshold to attack. But, the predictability of actions is not altered through public information compared to private information. The uncertainty caused by multiple equilibria has smaller effects than predicted by theory.

2. Model

2.1. Coordination Problem

I briefly review a creditor coordination game as analyzed by Morris and Shin (2004). A continuum of creditors provide the external financing for a firm. Together they hold the bonds, which account for the complete liabilities of the firm. If the firm survives, the repayment on bonds is 1. In case of default there is no repayment and the investment is lost. Default occurs if the intrinsic value of the firm θ is below a default point D, which is endogenously determined. The intrinsic value cannot be observed directly and is drawn by nature from an improper uniform prior. To make an assessment about the intrinsic value creditors use public and private information. Public information is the value of assets held by the firm $V_{A,T} = \theta + \eta_V$, where η_V is an error that is normally distributed with mean 0 and precision α. Additionally, every creditor draws conclusions about the intrinsic value resulting in a private signal $x_i = \theta + \varepsilon_i$, where ε_i is normally distributed with mean 0 and precision β.

At an intermediate state T creditors have the opportunity to review their investment. Creditors will foreclose if the private signal received indicates an intrinsic value θ that is worse than the default point D. These are all signals that lie below a threshold $x_i < x^*$. Hence, the fate of the firm is undetermined if the mass of foreclosing creditors l equals $\Pr\left(x_i < x^* \,|\theta = D\right)$. Thereby, the default point equals the fraction of creditors who can be redeemed. Hence, $D \in [0, 1]$. In equilibrium the mass of foreclosing creditors equals the default point $l = D$:

$$\Phi\left(\sqrt{\beta}\left(x^* - D\right)\right) = D, \tag{1}$$

where $\Phi\left(.\right)$ is the cumulative normal distribution. Thus, the default point D is selected implicitly through the investment decision.

To assess the fundamental state creditors build posterior beliefs by weighing the information received according to its precision:

$$\theta |\, V_{A,T}, x_i \sim N\left(\frac{\alpha V_{A,T} + \beta x_i}{\alpha + \beta}, \frac{1}{\sqrt{\alpha + \beta}}\right). \tag{2}$$

If a creditor chooses to foreclose on her bonds, she receives the market price p_{market}. Since each creditor is small, the market price is exogenous. If, however, the creditor rolls over, her expected payoff equals the survival probability of the firm $\Pr(\theta \geq D \,|V_{A,T}, x^*)$.[51] A creditor will therefore be indifferent if

$$1 - \Phi\left(\sqrt{\alpha+\beta}\left(D - \frac{\alpha V_{A,T} + \beta x^*}{\alpha+\beta}\right)\right) = p_{market}. \tag{3}$$

Solving (3) for x^* and inserting in (1) gives the equilibrium condition

$$D = \Phi\left(\frac{\alpha}{\sqrt{\beta}}\left(D - V_{A,T} + \Phi^{-1}\left(p_{market}\right)\frac{\sqrt{\alpha+\beta}}{\alpha}\right)\right), \tag{4}$$

where $\Phi^{-1}(.)$ is the inverse of the cumulative distribution function. Morris and Shin (2004) show that (4) has a unique solution if

$$\frac{\alpha}{\sqrt{\beta}} \leq \sqrt{2\pi}. \tag{5}$$

Naming the Merton model an empirical counterpart to the model presented, Morris and Shin (2004) suggest that it might be possible to compute the precision of public α and private β information if the data from the Merton model is connected to the coordination problem.[52]

2.2. Pricing of Debt

The coordination game implies two prices for the bond. Equation (3) gives the market price based on public and private information. However, it is also possible to calculate a price based solely on public information.

If the price of the bond equals the expected payoff, then no creditor has an incentive to buy or sell the bond, since both alternatives lead to the same expected payoff. With a repayment of either 0 or 1 the expected payoff equals the survival probability of the firm given a certain level of information $\Pr(\theta \geq D|\, I)$. The level of information I is either solely public information or private and public information.

The first price includes only public information and is therefore referred to as price

[51]The expected payoff equals the repayment in case of success times the survival probability plus the repayment in case of failure times the default probability, i.e. $1 \cdot \Pr(\theta \geq D\,|V_{A,T}, x^*) + 0 \cdot \Pr(\theta < D\,|V_{A,T}, x^*)$.

[52]This suggestion was the starting point for this paper. However, to compute the private information precision a model is needed that also extracts the default probability as perceived by the market. Therefore, I derive the default probability implied by CDS spreads.

forecast.[53] It equals the survival probability based on public information:

$$p_{forecast} = \Phi\left(\sqrt{\alpha}\left(V_{A,T} - D\right)\right). \tag{6}$$

To compute α I need the values of D, $V_{A,T}$ and $p_{forecast}$. The default point is firm-specific and time dependent. Therefore, I adopt the common assumption made in the literature that the default point equals the short-term debt plus half of the long-term debt (cf. Crouhy et al. 2003). Then the default point can be directly computed from the balance sheet of the firm. To get the asset value $V_{A,T}$ I use the Merton model (see section 2.3). Since the price forecast does not incorporate all information I cannot simply use a market price, rather I need a model that forecasts the price using the publicly available information. Hence, I use the KMV extension of the Merton model to get a forecast for the default probability, which is then discounted to yield the price forecast (see section 2.4).

The second price includes all information available and is therefore referred to as market price. It is obtained by calculating the survival probability conditional on public and private information:

$$p_{market} = \Phi\left(\sqrt{\alpha+\beta}\left(\frac{\alpha V_{A,T} + \beta x^*}{\alpha+\beta} - D\right)\right). \tag{3}$$

This equality is the indifference condition (3).[54]

To compute β I need the values of D, $V_{A,T}$, x^*, p_{market} and α. The default point and the asset value are obtained as before. Since the threshold signal x^* has no direct empirical counterpart, I present a different measure in the data section 3. Public information precision is obtained from (6). Since the market price includes all available information on bonds, it is derived from the implied default probability of CDS spreads (see section 2.5).

The KMV model as well as the CDS spreads give the default probability ρ of a bond maturing in one year. Since the payoff is normalized to 1 and the potential loss is 0, the price p equals the survival probability $1 - \rho$. Assuming there is a risk free investment alternative, the price of a bond can be written as:

$$p = (1 - \rho)\, exp\left(-r\right).$$

Discounting also assures finite values for the precision, even if the default probability becomes 1.

[53]Morris and Shin (2004) call it ex ante price.

[54]Here, I used the symmetry property of the normal distribution function: $1 - \Phi(x) = \Phi(-x)$.

As noted before, creditors decide upon rollover at an intermediate state T. This is the time when some creditors redeem their bonds. To calculate the prices for the bond, the time has to be specified. I consider a time horizon of one year. Therefore, I calculate annual default probabilities. Hence, a bond price states, what amount of money a creditor pays today for a repayment of 1 after one year, in case of success. I refer to time T as maturity date.

In the global game, default occurs if the intrinsic value is below the default point D. Since the default point equals the mass of foreclosing creditors it is restricted to the $[0, 1]$ interval. With debt and assets being denominated in the respective home currency of a firm it is necessary to find measures that are consistent with the global game formalization to solve equations (3) and (6). Therefore, I apply a firm specific scaling that divides both time series—default point and asset value—by the maximum of the asset value, i.e. $\frac{V_{A,T}}{max(V_{A,T})} = \widetilde{V}_A$ and $\frac{D}{max(V_{A,T})} = \widetilde{D}$. These scaled values are used instead of the original values in equations (3) and (6).

2.3. Value of Assets

To determine the value of assets $V_{A,T}$ I apply the option pricing approach of Merton (1974).[55] Compared to balance sheet data this approach has the advantage that it allows a daily estimation of the asset value based on the assessment of the market about equity, risk, and the perspective of the firm.[56] The starting point of the model is the option nature of equity. In a simplified balance sheet, assets are financed by equity and debt. Equity, as a subordinated claim, is the residual of assets and debt. Hence, only when the assets exceed the debt at maturity T the equity has value. The relevant level of debt that has to be backed by assets is the default point D. Hence, the equity value V_E at maturity T is

$$V_{E,T} = \max\left(V_{A,T} - D, 0\right), \tag{7}$$

which equals the price of a European call option: only if the underlying assets exceed the strike price (default point) at maturity the claim on equity has an inner value.[57]

The asset and equity value follow stochastic differential equations (cf. Merton 1974)

$$\frac{dV_A}{dt} = \left(\mu_A + \sigma_A \frac{dW}{dt}\right) V_A \tag{8}$$

[55] I use the standard assumptions of the Merton model.

[56] The approach uses the stock price (equity), the standard deviation of assets (risk), and the growth rate of assets (perspective).

[57] Note that a European call can only be exercised at maturity.

$$\frac{dV_E}{dt} = \left(\mu_E + \sigma_E \frac{dW}{dt}\right) V_E, \tag{9}$$

where W is a Wiener process, μ_A and μ_E are the instantaneous growth rates (drift), and σ_A and σ_E the standard deviations of assets and equity. Hence, the motion of assets and equity consists of a constant drift plus a stochastic variation.

The option nature of equity (7) makes it a function of the asset value and time $V_E = V_E(V_A, t)$. Thus, the motion of equity (9) depends also on the motion of assets (8). Therefore, the process followed by equity V_E is given by Itô's lemma (cf. Merton 1974):

$$\frac{dV_E}{dt} = \frac{1}{2}\frac{\partial^2 V_E}{\partial V_A^2}\sigma_A^2 V_A^2 + \frac{\partial V_E}{\partial V_A}\mu_A V_A + \frac{\partial V_E}{\partial t} + \frac{\partial V_E}{\partial V_A}\sigma_A V_A \frac{dW}{dt} \tag{10}$$

Note that, by assumption, the asset value as well as the equity value share the same stochastic component dW. Therefore, it is possible to construct a portfolio, that involves selling 1 unit of equity and buying $\frac{\partial V_E}{\partial V_A}$ units of assets,[58] in which the instantaneous risk is eliminated (cf. Hull 2012). With the boundary conditions—(i) if the asset value is zero, the equity value is zero $V_E(0, t) = 0$; (ii) the equity value is always greater or equal zero $V_E \geq 0$ and (iii) at maturity equity is $V_E(V_A, T) = \max(0, V_{A,T} - D)$—this portfolio leads to a partial differential equation that gives the Black-Scholes-Merton formula (cf. Merton 1974):

$$V_E = V_A \Phi(d_1) - D \exp(-r) \Phi(d_2) \tag{11}$$

with

$$d_1 \equiv \frac{\ln V_A - \ln D + r + \frac{\sigma_A^2}{2}}{\sigma_A}$$

$$d_2 \equiv \frac{\ln V_A - \ln D + r - \frac{\sigma_A^2}{2}}{\sigma_A} = d_1 - \sigma_A,$$

where r is the risk free interest rate.[59]

Except from the asset value V_A and the standard deviation of assets σ_A all variables in (11) are observable. Therefore, a second equation is needed to compute V_A and σ_A. Through comparing the stochastic terms in equations (9) and (10) a relation between the standard deviations of equity and assets is obtained (cf. Merton 1974):

$$\sigma_E V_E = \frac{\partial V_E}{\partial V_A} \sigma_A V_A.$$

[58]Buying $\frac{\partial V_E}{\partial V_A}$ units of assets, according to (8), leads to an instantaneous risk of $\frac{\partial V_E}{\partial V_A}\sigma_A V_A \frac{dW}{dt}$, while selling 1 unit of equity, according to (10), leads to an instantaneous risk of $-\frac{\partial V_E}{\partial V_A}\sigma_A V_A \frac{dW}{dt}$. In a portfolio both risk components cancel out.

[59]With the portfolio being riskless, r is used as discount factor.

The derivative $\frac{\partial V_E}{\partial V_A}$ shows the change in the equity value for an infinitesimal change in the asset value. This relation is also known as the delta Δ of an option. In the appendix I show that $\frac{\partial V_E}{\partial V_A} = \Phi(d_1)$. Hence, the relation of the standard deviations can be written as (cf. Crosbie and Bohn, 2003)

$$\sigma_E = \Phi(d_1)\,\sigma_A \frac{V_A}{V_E}. \tag{12}$$

2.4. Forecasting the Probability of Default

To assess the default probability of the firm I use the KMV extension of the Merton model as described in a Moody's paper by Crosbie and Bohn (2003), which was adapted to empirical studies, e.g. Vassalou and Xing (2004) or Bharath and Shumway (2008).

When the firm cannot repay its debt default occurs. That is, if the asset value is below the default point at the time of maturity T. Hence, the default probability ρ_{KMV} is $\Pr(V_{A,T} < D | V_{A,0})$, where $V_{A,0}$ indicates the initial asset value. In logarithmic notation the default probability is

$$\rho_{KMV} = \Pr(\ln V_{A,T} < \ln D | \ln V_{A,0}), \tag{13}$$

where the motion of $\ln V_A$ can be obtained by applying Itô's lemma to equation (8): $d \ln V_A = \left(\mu_A - \frac{\sigma_A^2}{2}\right) dt + \sigma_A dW$ (cf. Hull 2012). The Wiener process is equivalent to a randomly drawn number from a normal distribution in a small time period $dW = \varepsilon\sqrt{dt}$. With ε being iid, the value of the stochastic component at maturity is $\varepsilon\sqrt{T}$. Hence, the logarithmic asset value at maturity is

$$\ln V_{A,T} = \ln V_{A,0} + \left(\mu_A - \frac{\sigma_A^2}{2}\right) T + \sigma_A \varepsilon \sqrt{T}. \tag{14}$$

Inserting (14) in (13) and rearranging gives

$$\rho_{KMV} = \Pr\left(-\frac{\ln V_{A,0} + \left(\mu_A - \frac{\sigma_A^2}{2}\right) T - \ln D}{\sigma_A \sqrt{T}} > \varepsilon\right),$$

which can be computed as cumulative distribution function (cdf)

$$\rho_{kmv} = \Phi\left(-\frac{\ln V_{A,0} + \left(\mu_A - \frac{\sigma_A^2}{2}\right) T - \ln D}{\sigma_A \sqrt{T}}\right). \tag{15}$$

The argument of the cdf measures the difference between assets and the default point in standard units of the fluctuation of assets. Therefore, the argument is termed distance to default DD.

Now that I have a model that gives a forecast for the default probability I have an alternative method to compute the price forecast of a standardized bond:

$$p_{forecast} = (1 - \rho_{kmv})\, exp\,(-r)\,.$$

Equating the price obtained from the default probability given by the option price model with the price forecast obtained from the coordination game (6) I can solve for the precision of public information:

$$(1 - \rho_{kmv})\, exp\,(-r) = \Phi\left(\sqrt{\alpha}\left(\widetilde{V}_A - \widetilde{D}\right)\right). \tag{16}$$

Note that in the global game equation on the right hand side I take account of the scaled values $\widetilde{V}_A$ and $\widetilde{D}$.

2.5. Market Implied Probability of Default

Bond holders can protect themselves from a default of the issuer through buying a credit default swap (CDS). The bond holder acquires the right to sell an amount of bonds specified in the contract at face value if the issuer defaults. In turn the seller has the obligation to buy the bonds at face value. For the right to sell, the buyer pays the seller a periodic fee that is denominated in basis points and is called spread (cf. Hull 2012). A contract is typically concluded for five years.[60]

In case of default, the seller buys the bonds at face value and can only redeem them at the recovery rate R. If the face value is normalized to 1, the loss arising is $1 - R$. For this protection the buyer pays the spread s per year. I adopt the typical assumptions from the literature that defaults occur only in the middle of the year and payments are made semiannually (cf. Hull 2012). Moreover, the annual default probability ρ_{cds} is assumed to be constant.

In case of no default the protection buyer pays the spread every year. The according annual survival probability is $(1 - \rho_{cds})$. For a notional value of 1 the annual payment is $\frac{s}{100}$.[61] If the payment is made at years end starting from today, the present value of the expected payments is $\frac{s}{100} \sum_{t=1}^{5} (1 - \rho_{cds})^t \exp(-rt)$.

[60] Other time spans are possible, but five year CDS are the most liquid.

[61] The spread s is denominated in basis points. When considering the cash flow, $\frac{s}{100}$ times the notional value 1 is payed.

If a default occurs, the protection seller pays a compensation in amount of the loss $1-R$. The default probability in a given year is conditional on that no default has taken place before: $\rho_{cds}\left(1-\rho_{cds}\right)^{t-1}$. Since it is assumed that defaults happen only in the middle of the year the discount factor is $\exp\left(-r\left(t-\frac{1}{2}\right)\right)$, which is used to calculate the present value of the payoff to the protection buyer: $(1-R)\sum_{t=1}^{5}\rho_{cds}\left(1-\rho_{cds}\right)^{t-1}\exp\left(-r\left(t-\frac{1}{2}\right)\right)$. In a year with a default the normal spread is not paid but an accrual payment is made till a default occurs. Due to the assumption that defaults only occur in the middle of the year half of the spread is paid $\frac{1}{2}\frac{s}{100}$. The probability of default is again conditional on that there was no earlier default: $\rho_{cds}\left(1-\rho_{cds}\right)^{t-1}$. The present value of the accrual payment is therefore $\frac{1}{2}\frac{s}{100}\sum_{t=1}^{5}\rho_{cds}\left(1-\rho_{cds}\right)^{t-1}\exp\left(-r\left(t-\frac{1}{2}\right)\right)$.

Equating the present value of payments made by the protection buyer with the present value of the payments made by the protection seller gives:

$$\frac{s}{100}\sum_{t=1}^{5}\left(1-\rho_{cds}\right)^{t}\exp\left(-rt\right)+\frac{1}{2}\frac{s}{100}\sum_{t=1}^{5}\rho_{cds}\left(1-\rho_{cds}\right)^{t-1}\exp\left(-r\left(t-\frac{1}{2}\right)\right)=$$
$$(1-R)\sum_{t=1}^{5}\rho_{cds}\left(1-\rho_{cds}\right)^{t-1}\exp\left(-r\left(t-\frac{1}{2}\right)\right) \tag{17}$$

The equation states that the expected payment plus the accrual payment equals the expected payoff. Since the spread and the interest rate are observable, the time horizon is known, and the recovery rate is assumed, the default probability ρ_{cds}, implied by the CDS, can be calculated. I will also refer to this probability as market default probability.

Again the survival probability $1-\rho_{cds}$ is discounted with the risk free interest rate r to yield a bond price with face value 1:

$$p_{market}=\left(1-\rho_{cds}\right)exp\left(-r\right)$$

Equating the price obtained from the default probability implied by the CDS spreads with the market price (3), obtained from the coordination game, I can solve for the precision of private information β:

$$\left(1-\rho_{cds}\right)exp\left(-r\right)=\Phi\left(\sqrt{\alpha+\beta}\left(\frac{\alpha\widetilde{V}_A+\beta x^*}{\alpha+\beta}-\widetilde{D}\right)\right). \tag{18}$$

Again I take account of the scaled values $\widetilde{V}_A$ and $\widetilde{D}$.

3. Data and Computation

I use daily market data from Thomson Reuters (Datastream) with a time horizon from 1999-2012 for a sample of 13 automotive firms.[62] I choose the automotive sector because it is a consolidated sector with a distinct number of firms that cover the range from healthy balance sheet to default event. Stock prices are from the respective home stock market of the company. The balance sheet data consists of short-term debt, which refers to all borrowings that are repayable within one year (datastream code 309). I use total debt (code 1301) to calculate the long-term debt as difference between total debt and short-term debt. The number of outstanding shares is computed as ratio of total sales (code 104) and sales per share (code 1505). US Treasury Bill returns with a maturity of 1 year are used as the risk free interest rate. I use five year CDS spreads from Bloomberg as far as available in the database.

The sequence of the computations is as follows:

1. Observations V_E and σ_E are used to compute the asset value V_A and its standard deviation σ_A from the Merton model
2. The KMV model states that the difference of assets and debt at maturity determines the default probability. Discounting finally yields the price forecast $p_{forecast}$
3. The precision of public information α is calculated
4. CDS spreads determine the default probability implied by the market and hence the market price p_{market}
5. The precision of private information β is calculated

In the remainder of the chapter I will work through the steps and present the results for Daimler. The results for all firms are presented in the next chapter and the plots are given in the appendix.

Merton Model To solve the Merton model (11) and (12) for the asset value V_A and the standard deviation of assets σ_A, I need the risk free interest rate r, the equity value V_E, the standard deviation of equity σ_E, and the default point D.

[62]The firms are: BMW, Daimler, Fiat, Ford, Honda, Hyundai, Mazda, Nissan, Peugeot, Renault, Tata, Toyota, VW.

The equity value V_E equals the stock price multiplied by the number of outstanding shares. From the equity time series, I calculate daily values of the annual standard deviation in percentage points of the equity value σ_E. Crosbie and Bohn (2003) state that the default point D lies between the short-term debt and the total debt. Crouhy et al. (2000) concretize the default point to be the short-term debt plus half of the long-term debt. This evolved as the standard approach, which was adopted by the literature, cf. e.g. Vassalou and Xing (2004) and others.

A joint solution of (11) and (12) gives the asset value V_A and the standard deviation of assets σ_A. However, Crosbie and Bohn (2003) argue that results obtained from (12) aren't reasonable, since the equation holds only instantaneously. As alternative, they propose an iterative procedure. Therefore, I rewrite the equations (11) and (12) as functions in terms of V_A and σ_A and equate them to 0:

$$g\left(V_A{}^i \middle| \sigma_A^i\right) = V_E - V_A{}^i \Phi\left(d_1\right) + D \exp\left(-r\right) \Phi\left(d_2\right) = 0 \tag{19}$$

$$h\left(\sigma_A^{i+1} \middle| V_A{}^i\right) = \sigma_E - \Phi\left(d_1\right) \sigma_A^{i+1} \frac{V_A{}^i}{V_E} = 0 \tag{20}$$

To find the roots I apply the uniroot function from the R package, which uses Brent's method. I use σ_E as initial value of σ_A^i to compute $V_A{}^i$ from (19) and then use it to compute σ_A^{i+1} from (20). σ_A^{i+1} then replaces σ_A^i in (19) to compute a new value $V_A{}^{i+1}$ in the second iteration. This procedure is repeated till σ_A converges, that is if the difference of two consecutive values σ_A^{i+1} and σ_A^i is below 10^{-4}.[63] The converged value of σ_A is used to compute the final value of V_A. The obtained values of V_A and σ_A are the solutions to (11) and (12). For Daimler the standard deviation converges after three iterations.

Figure (III.1) shows the outcome of the iteration. Panel (a) relates the asset value to the equity value and the default point. Characteristic is the increase in equity and assets before the crisis and the subsequent reduction. Panel (b) shows the standard deviations of equity and assets. Including debt, assets have a lower variability, especially during times of crisis.

The evaluation through the option price model allows a daily market based assessment of risk. It incorporates changes in the perception of risk of market participants but is therefore prone to exaggerations.

Forecasting the Probability of Default The firm defaults if the asset value is less than the default point at maturity. The default point is the short-term debt plus half the long-term debt and is directly obtained from the balance sheet.

From the Merton model I know the current asset value but I need the value of assets at

[63] The absoulte difference of 10^{-4} equals $\frac{1}{60}$ of the minimum standard deviation of assets in the sample.

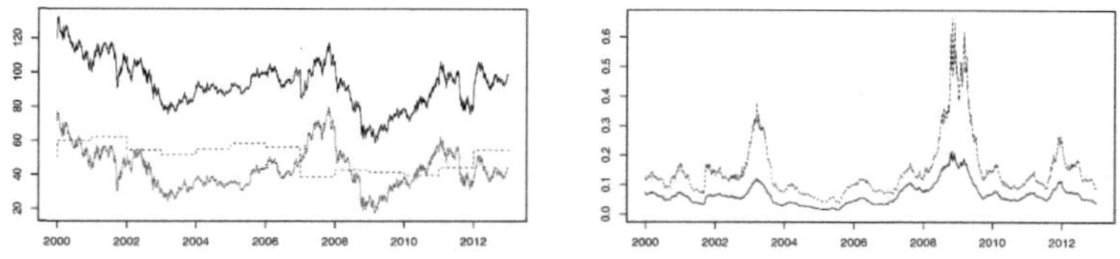

(a) Balance Sheet (b) Standard Deviations

Figure III.1.: **Results of the Merton model for Daimler:** Panel (a) shows the asset value (continuous), the equity value (dotted), and the default point (dashed), which are denominated in Euro. Panel (b) shows the standard deviations of assets (continuous) and equity (dashed), which are denominated relative to the value of assets and equity.

maturity in one year. Assuming a log normal distribution (14) the expected asset value at maturity depends on the initial value plus the annual growth rate minus half the variance of assets. While the literature agrees on the computation of the variance through the iteration procedure, it differs on the computation of the annual growth rate. Crosbie and Bohn (2003) only state that μ is the 'expected return on the firm's assets' but do not give a computation method. Bharath and Shumway (2008) use the asset value to calculate an 'implied log return on assets each day' and claim to use this to estimate new values of the asset volatility and the asset return via the Merton model. However, the Merton model does not include the asset return and thus it is unclear to what 'estimate' refers to. The computation is reasonable after the iteration converged. But if Bharat and Shumway then use the daily log return, they obtain a value of assets at maturity that depends to much on daily fluctuations of the equity market. Vassalou and Xing (2004) compute the return as the mean of the change of the logarithmic asset value, where neither the time horizon of the change nor the mean is specified.

The problem is that the daily asset value is too volatile. Especially in boom or bust situations annual growth rates of 100% or more are obtained, so that results aren't reasonable. In contrast to the literature, I decided to use the five year average of the annualized log return on assets as annual growth rate.

With the asset return being randomly distributed around $V_{A,T}$, the difference between the assets and the default point is measured in standard units and is called distance to default (cf. equation 15).

Figure III.2[64] shows the absolute value of the distance to default of Daimler that is used

[64]Since the CDS spreads are only available form 2005 onwards I reduce the time frame for all following plots.

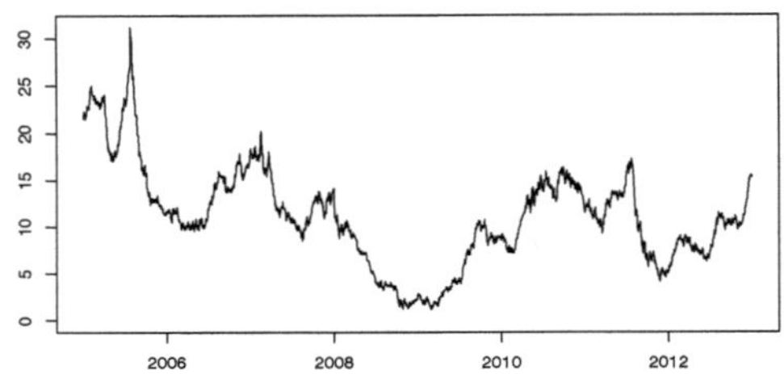

Figure III.2.: Distance to default of Daimler in standard units

as argument in the cumulative normal distribution to compute the default probability. In the original version by KMV, once the distance to default is obtained, companies having the same distance to default values are selected from a historic database. The fraction of companies, in the selection that defaulted, is a measure for the default probability.[65] This empirical distribution of defaults has fat tails, i.e. firms with a distance to default of 4 still have a probability of default of about 1% (cf. Crosbie and Bohn 2003) compared to 0.0032% obtained from the normal distribution. Having no access to a historic database covering thousands of defaults, I follow the literature (e.g. Vassalou and Xing 2004) and use a normal distribution (15) to obtain a measure for the default probability.

Once I have the forecasted default probability I can calculate a daily price forecast for a standardized bond with repayment 1. This gives the left hand side of (16). Inserting the scaled variables $\widetilde{V}_A$ and $\widetilde{D}$ then allows to solve for the precision of public information α:

$$(1-\rho_{KMV})\,exp\,(-r)=\Phi\left(\sqrt{\alpha}\left(\widetilde{V}_A-\widetilde{D}\right)\right). \tag{16}$$

To compute $\widetilde{V}_A$ I need the value of assets at maturity $V_{A,T}$, which equals the expected value of (14) $V_{A,T}=exp\,(ln\,(V_{A,T}))$.

Market Implied Probability of Default Having determined the price forecast for the standardized bond I yet need its market price. To compute the market price, I discount the annual default probability implied by five year CDS spreads according to (17).

To solve (17) I need to define the recovery rate, which determines the actual repayment to the creditors. The literature typically assumes a constant recovery rate of 0.4 (cf. Hull 2012). The assumption of the recovery rate is crucial for the calculation of the default probability. Since a standard exists that is widely accepted by market participants, I

[65]KMV calls this fraction expected default frequency.

utilize it to compute the default probability implied by the market. Moreover, I assume that the risk free rate r is fixed over time, so I use one year T-Bills for discounting. With a definite time horizon of five years and the spread being observable the default probability ρ_{cds} implied by the CDS spreads can be calculated.

I use the discounted survival probability to retrieve the market price. To determine the precision of private information from (18) I have to find another measure for the threshold signal x^*, which has no direct empirical counterpart. However, the difference $x^* - D$ measures the distance between the equilibrium beliefs and the default point. I interpret this measure as the distance to default DD. Inserting in (18) and rearranging gives:[66]

$$p_{market} = \Phi\left(\frac{\alpha}{\sqrt{\alpha+\beta}}\left(\widetilde{V}_A - \widetilde{D} + \frac{\beta}{\alpha}\widetilde{DD}\right)\right). \tag{21}$$

Obviously, as noted in section 2.2 the distance to default has to be scaled if it is used in the global game formalization. Hence, $\widetilde{DD} = \frac{DD}{max(V_{A,T})}$.

For $\widetilde{V}_A \geq \widetilde{D}$ the cdf on the right hand side in equations (16) and (21) takes a value of $[0.5, 1]$. Hence, there is only a solution for α and β for prices higher than 0.5.

The resulting default probability, market price, and precision of private information for Daimler are plotted in figure III.3.

It is striking that private β and public α information precision follow the respective evolution of the price. However the difference of assets and default point can't be neglected. As well as the influence of the public precision on the private precision. The middle panel shows the evolution of the market price (dotted) and the forecasted price (solid). From 2009, with the interest rate approaching zero, the evolution of the prices just mirrors the evolution of the default probabilities. Before, a small risk spread is observable.

An important distinction between the precision of public and private information is the different evolution of the forecasted default probability and the market default probability (cf. upper panel of figure III.3). Differences can be due to the structure of debt, the growth rate of assets, the variability of assets, or the recovery rate.

Apparently, due to the normal distribution, default is less likely than under an empirical distribution as used by Moody's. In reality, the default point might increase rapidly before a default, so that assuming a constant default point underestimates the default probability in cases of rising indebtedness. Then, the dependency upon balance sheet data, that is only available with a time lag, is also a problem. The variation in the return on assets is problematic in the sense that before a crisis, stock prices frequently rise which can actually lower the default probability even if the default point increases.

[66] A detailed derivation is given in the appendix.

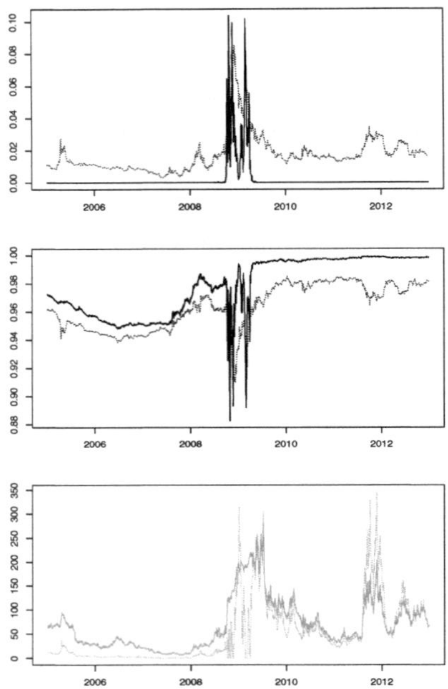

Figure III.3.: **Default probabilities, prices, and precision of Daimler:** The upper panel shows the forecasted (black) and the market (dotted) default probabilities. In the middle panel the forecasted (black) and market (dotted) prices are given. The lower panel shows the precision of public (gray) and private (dotted) information.

4. Results and Discussion

First, I present and summarize the stylized facts of the balance sheet data and the Merton model for the automotive firms. Then I discuss the default probabilities and implied prices and show how these influence the precision. Finally, I describe the influencing factors of the relative precision. Plots of the time series are given in the appendix.

Balance Sheet and the Merton Model Before the subprime crisis, the equity value of most automotive firms increased with a peak in late 2007 (cf. figure III.4). During the crisis the equity value dropped to lows in the region of the last recession 2003. After the minimum in October 2008 equity values stabilized and recovered. Notable exceptions form this development are Ford, which had severe problems over the complete decade and VW, which was mainly influenced by the takeover attempt of Porsche in 2008.

The characteristics of the default point are rather firm specific. However, the default point of most firms consolidates after the crisis.

The asset value follows the equity value. Note that here the current asset value is considered, while for the computation of the default probability the asset value at maturity is used.

The standard deviations (SD) of assets and equities peak in February 2009 for most firms (cf. figure III.5). The date corresponds to the low in the stock market. The European firms exhibit a second increase in late 2011. Ford is the only firm with a clearly dominating double peak in its SD in November 2008 and May 2009 shortly after its default on April 6th 2009 (cf. Standard and Poors 2010).

With debt having a low variability, the SD of assets is lower than the SD of equity. Especially during crisis when the stock market becomes very volatile the difference in SDs between assets and equity grows.

Default Probabilities and Prices All companies exhibit a peak in their default probability (PD) in February 2009 (cf. figure III.8). In more detail the market PD increases during the crisis for every firm, while BMW, Honda, Hyundai, and Toyota have forecasted PDs near zero during the crisis. This was due to a comfortable distance between the assets and the default point (cf. figure III.7) and a low asset volatility compared to the other companies. Only Hyundai had a lower distance, but this was compensated by strong asset growth.

VW is again an exception. Its market PD increased slightly during the crisis, while the forecasted PD rose not until late 2009, when the market PD had already fallen to its precrisis level.

For Mazda, Nissan, Peugeot, and Renault the forecasted PD strongly exceeded the market PD during the crisis. These firms suffered from a short distance between the assets and the default point accompanied with high asset volatility and negative asset growth rates (cf. figure III.6). Fiat and Peugeot exhibit a second increase in late 2011. This was caused by a lower distance between the assets and the default point as well as a high asset volatility. Fiat additionally had a negative asset growth.

The forecasted PD has the advantage over ratings that it allows a daily assessment of the perceived risk by the market. However, the forecast is therefore prone to the exaggerations of the market. The strong increase in VW's stock price during the crisis, due to the takeover attempt of Porsche led to a PD near zero. While when the attempt failed and stock prices plumped the forecasted PD rose. Both events happened in a years time span when the fundamental situation did not change substantially. Another problem when comparing the market PD and the forecasted PD is the assumption of a normally distributed default probability. This neglects fat tails, so that for high distance to default measures the PD is underestimated, while for low measures the PD is overestimated. Therefore, during tranquil periods the actual PD is higher, while during a crisis the actual PD is lower than the one computed by the normal distribution.

Discounting the default probabilities with the T-Bill returns gives the prices for the standardized bond. Figure III.9 shows the forecasted and the market price. With the T-Bill return being below 1% from October 2008 the prices mirror the default probability. The bow between 2005 and 2008, which is best visible for firms with low PDs, is due to the rise and fall of the T-Bill return.

Precision of Information In the tranquil period before the crisis public information precision α exceeded private information precision β for all firms (cf. figure III.10). Interestingly, the crisis as a singular event is only noticeable in the precision plots of BMW, Daimler, Ford, Honda, Hyundai, and Tata. In contrast to the tranquil period, here, private information precision β mainly exceeded public information precision α.

Fiat, Mazda, Peugeot, Renault, and VW do not show any sign of a crisis in 2009, with their precision remaining flat. For Fiat, Mazda, Peugeot, and Renault the current asset value was near or below the default point. Accompanied by high PDs (low prices) this results in low precision values (16) and (21). On the other hand, VW exhibited a large distance between assets and the default point with a low PD, which also results in low precision values.

The Japanese and most of the European firms have an equal or even larger increase in absolute precision after 2012. Thereby, (i) Fiat, Mazda, and Renault have a higher β and (ii) Honda, Nissan, Peugeot, Toyota, and VW exhibit alternating increases in α and β. Mazda and Renault had relatively low PDs after 2012 where the market PD exceeded the forecasted PD. However, the distance between assets and the default point reduced so that α and β increased. In the end of 2011 the forecasted PD of Fiat increased rapidly due to a deterioration of the balance sheet and additionally an increase in the SD. As noted earlier, the low distance between the assets and the default point accompanied by a high PD lowers the precision. In early 2012 the SD fell and the distance increased so that the PD dropped. Since the forecasted PD dropped to around zero an adaption in α was necessary, which rose accordingly.

Honda, Nissan, Toyota, and VW have reduced PDs after the crisis. Their market PD is at a level slightly higher than before the crisis. In 2012 Peugeot's distance between the assets and the default point fell and additionally its SD increased. The result was a strong increase of the forecasted PD that exceeded the market PD in April 2012. Thereby, public information precision rose, while private information became imprecise. The impact of increases in the forecasted PD on the precision is illustrated in more detail in the next paragraph.

Relative Precision and Multiple Equilibria Morris and Shin (2004) state that the equilibrium is unique if the precision of private information is sufficiently high compared to the precision of public information (cf. equation 5). In this case creditors' beliefs are dispersed so that they cannot coordinate on different equilibria. However, if the precision of public information increases, beliefs are less dispersed, coordination is facilitated, and multiple equilibria emerge.

To show whether multiple equilibria are more likely I show how the relative precision of public and private information $\frac{\beta}{\alpha}$ evolves. To analyze the causes for the evolution of the relative precision I also plot the forecasted and the market default probabilities in the same figure. For illustration purposes, that allow an easy comparison with the PDs, I scale the relative precision by its maximum. Hence, $\widetilde{\frac{\beta}{\alpha}} = \frac{\beta}{\alpha}/max\frac{\beta}{\alpha}$ is plotted in figure III.11. The dashed horizontal line shows where $\beta = \alpha$.

Considering the relative precision, it is striking that it follows the market PD and plumps whenever the forecasted PD rises. Figure III.12 zooms in on periods when the forecasted PD increased significantly.[67] Hence, if risk is forecasted but not accounted for in the market, then creditors put barely weight on private information and build their posterior belief mainly on public information.

The relative precision $\frac{\beta}{\alpha}$ rises if an increase in the market PD is not captured in the forecasted PD. Then creditors weigh private information more than public information. Coordination is hampered and multiple equilibria become less likely.

Relative precision declines if an increase in the forecasted PD is not followed by the market PD. In this situation creditors weigh public information more than private information. Coordination is facilitated and multiple equilibria become more likely.

In sum, multiple equilibria are more likely if forecasts of the default probability are not incorporated by market reactions. While, unique equilibria are more likely if forecasts do not show the increase in the market default probability.

Summary and Conclusion Even though the Merton model is build on variety of assumptions and scaling of the observed variables is necessary to fit in the normal distribution formalization of the global game, the main results are robust. That is, the relative precision of private to public information rises if an increase in the default probability implied by the market is not forecasted. On the other hand, the relative precision falls if a forecasted increase in the default probability is not reflected in the market. Thus, multiple equilibria are most likely in situations where forecasts of increased risk are not incorporated in market prices.

In reality, beliefs evolve over time. While forecasts do not include all available information, deviations from market prices are necessary if the informational content is time dependent. Hence, the literature that uses prices as information aggregates neglects the difference between forecasts and market prices. Considering the price as information aggregate and neglecting the information processing prevents from finding the cause of multiple equilibria. Depending on the precision, the market price can be the result of mainly private information as well as mainly public information with a completely contrasting likelihood for the emergence of multiple equilibria.

[67] Missing values in the relative precision are due to prices below 0.5 for which no solution for the precision is possible.

5. Appendix

Option Δ To find an expression for the option's delta I differentiate the equity value (11) with respect to the asset value:

$$\frac{\partial V_E}{\partial V_{A,T}} = \Phi(d_1) + V_{A,T}\phi(d_1)\frac{1}{\sigma_A V_{A,T}} - D\exp(-r)\phi(d_2)\frac{1}{\sigma_A V_{A,T}}, \tag{22}$$

where $\phi(.)$ is the standard normal density function with $\phi(d_1) = \frac{1}{\sqrt{2\pi}}\exp\left(-\frac{1}{2}{d_1}^2\right)$. Note that $d_1 = d_2 + \sigma_A$ (cf. 11). I rewrite $\phi(d_1)$ in terms of the exponential representation and d_2

$$\phi(d_1) = \frac{1}{\sqrt{2\pi}}\exp\left(-\frac{1}{2}(d_2+\sigma_A)^2\right),$$

expand the binomial

$$\phi(d_1) = \frac{1}{\sqrt{2\pi}}\exp\left(-\frac{1}{2}\left({d_2}^2 + 2d_2\sigma_A + \sigma_A^2\right)\right)$$

and rearrange, to get:

$$\phi(d_1) = \frac{1}{\sqrt{2\pi}}\exp\left(-\frac{1}{2}{d_2}^2\right)\exp\left(-d_2\sigma_A - \frac{1}{2}\sigma_A^2\right).$$

The first exponential function is again written in terms of the density function $\phi(.)$ and in the second exponential function the expression for d_2 is inserted

$$\phi(d_1) = \phi(d_2)\exp\left(-\left(\frac{\ln V_{A,T} - \ln D + \left(r - \frac{\sigma_A^2}{2}\right)}{\sigma_A}\right)\sigma_A - \frac{1}{2}\sigma_A^2\right).$$

Expanding gives

$$\phi(d_1) = \phi(d_2)\exp(-\ln V_{A,T} + \ln D - r),$$

which equals:

$$\phi(d_1) = \phi(d_2)\frac{D}{V_{A,T}}\exp(-r).$$

Inserted in (22) gives

$$\frac{\partial V_E}{\partial V_{A,T}} = \Phi(d_1) + V_{A,T}\phi(d_2)\frac{D}{V_{A,T}}\exp(-r)\frac{1}{\sigma_A V_{A,T}} - D\exp(-r)\phi(d_2)\frac{1}{\sigma_A V_{A,T}},$$

which equals:

$$\frac{\partial V_E}{\partial V_{A,T}} = \Phi(d_1) \equiv \Delta.$$

Threshold signal

$$(1-\rho_{CDS})\exp(-r) = \Phi\left(\sqrt{\alpha+\beta}\left(\frac{\alpha V_{A,T}+\beta x^*}{\alpha+\beta} - D\right)\right) \tag{18}$$

Since the threshold signal x^* from equation (18) has no direct empirical counterpart I subtract the default point $x^* - D$ to obtain

$$p_{market} = \Phi\left(\sqrt{\alpha+\beta}\left(\frac{\alpha V_{A,T}+\beta(x^*-D)+\beta D}{\alpha+\beta} - D\right)\right).$$

I equate $x^* - D = DD$ and rearrange

$$p_{market} = \Phi\left(\sqrt{\alpha+\beta}\left(\frac{\alpha V_{A,T}}{\alpha+\beta} + \frac{\beta DD}{\alpha+\beta} + \frac{\beta D - (\alpha+\beta)D}{\alpha+\beta}\right)\right),$$

factor out

$$\Phi\left(\frac{1}{\sqrt{\alpha+\beta}}(\alpha V_{A,T} + \beta DD - \alpha D)\right),$$

and get

$$\Phi\left(\frac{\alpha}{\sqrt{\alpha+\beta}}\left(V_{A,T} + \frac{\beta}{\alpha}DD - D\right)\right). \tag{21}$$

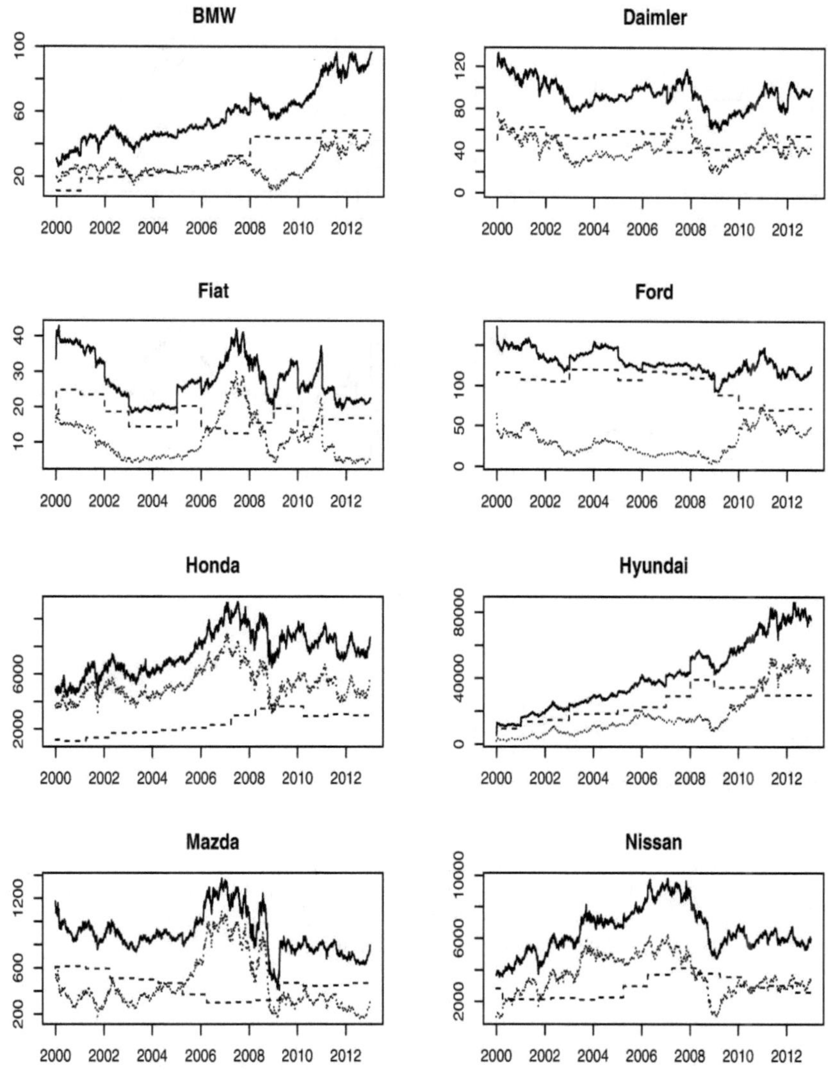
BMW
20
60
100
2000 2002 2004 2006 2008 2010 2012
Daimler
0
40
80
120
2000 2002 2004 2006 2008 2010 2012
Fiat
10
20
30
40
2000 2002 2004 2006 2008 2010 2012
Ford
0
50
100
2000 2002 2004 2006 2008 2010 2012
Honda
2000
6000
2000 2002 2004 2006 2008 2010 2012
Hyundai
0
40000
80000
2000 2002 2004 2006 2008 2010 2012
Mazda
200
600
1200
2000 2002 2004 2006 2008 2010 2012
Nissan
2000
6000
10000
2000 2002 2004 2006 2008 2010 2012

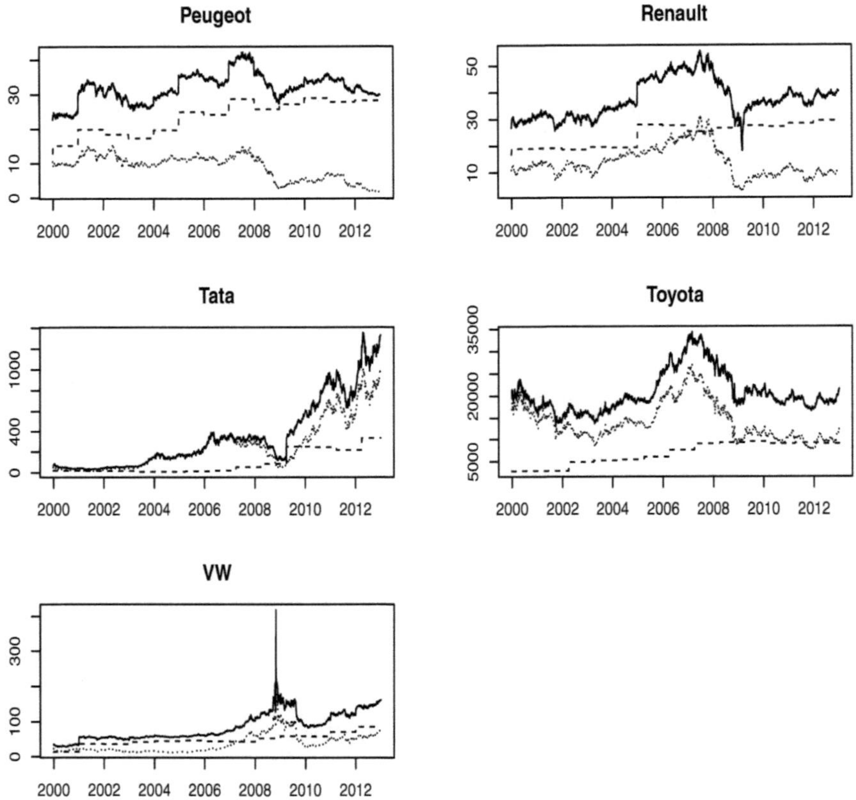

Figure III.4.: **Blance sheet and the Merton model:** The equity value (dotted) equals the shares outstanding times the stock price. The default point (dashed) is the short-term debt plus half the long-term debt. The asset value (solid) is given by the Merton model. Data is denominated in the respective home currency. Note that, in Japan, the fiscal year ends on 31st March.

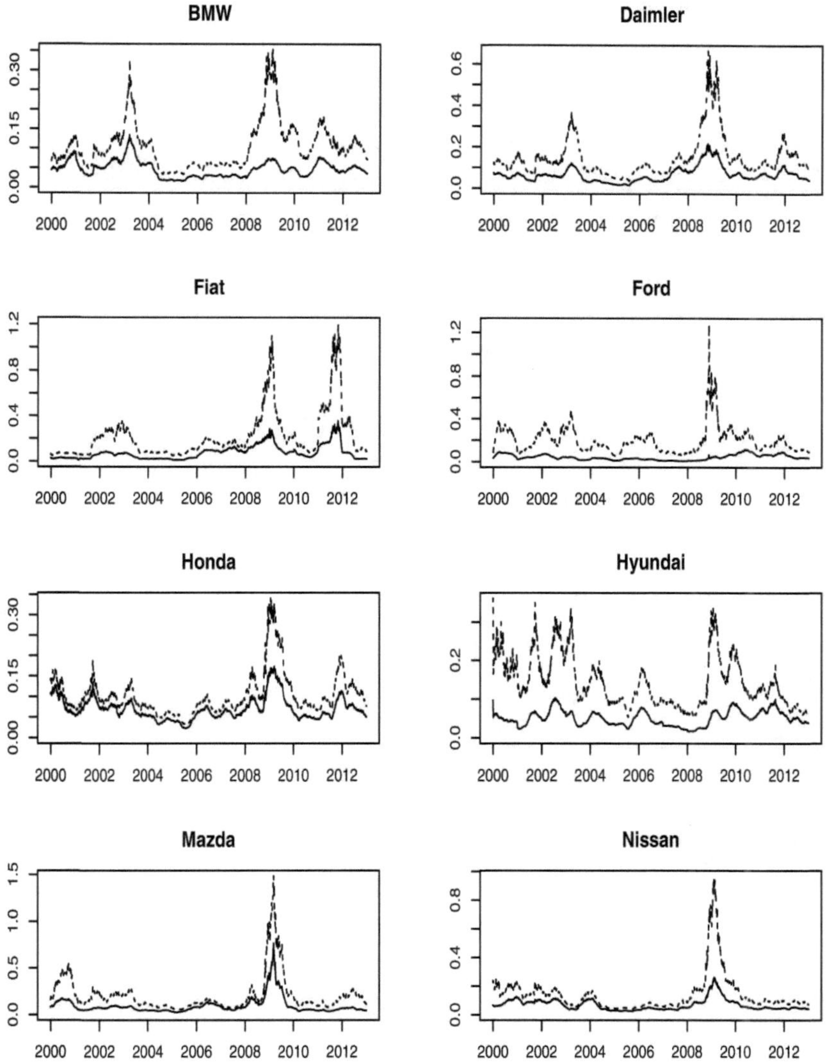
BMW
0.00
0.15
0.30
2000 2002 2004 2006 2008 2010 2012
Daimler
0.0
0.2
0.4
0.6
2000 2002 2004 2006 2008 2010 2012
Fiat
0.0
0.4
0.8
1.2
2000 2002 2004 2006 2008 2010 2012
Ford
0.0
0.4
0.8
1.2
2000 2002 2004 2006 2008 2010 2012
Honda
0.00
0.15
0.30
2000 2002 2004 2006 2008 2010 2012
Hyundai
0.0
0.2
2000 2002 2004 2006 2008 2010 2012
Mazda
0.0
0.5
1.0
1.5
2000 2002 2004 2006 2008 2010 2012
Nissan
0.0
0.4
0.8
2000 2002 2004 2006 2008 2010 2012

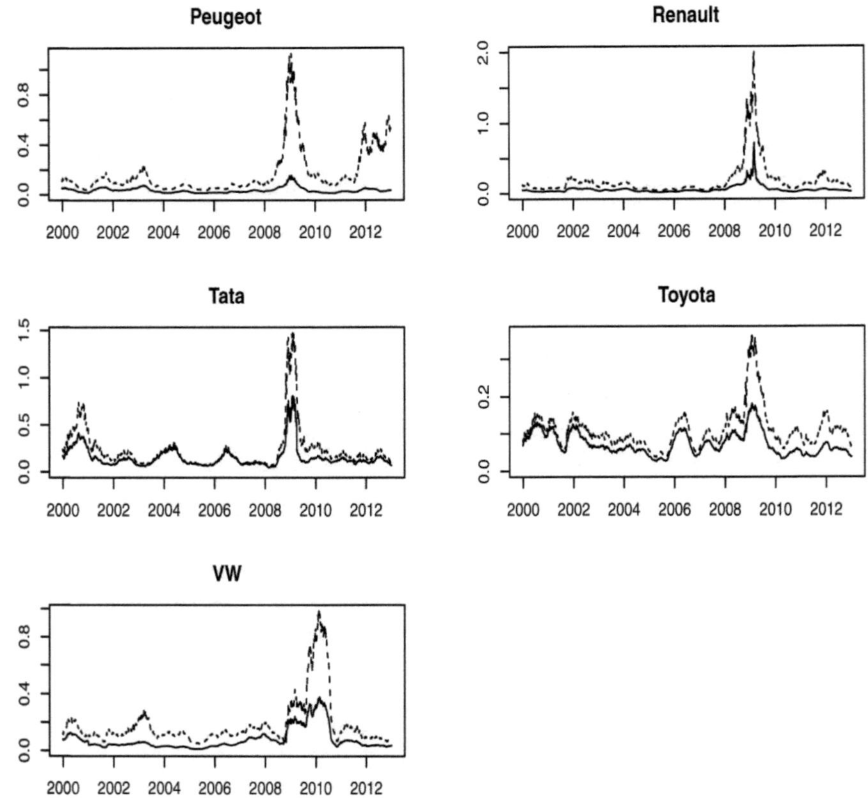

Figure III.5.: **Volatility:** The figure shows the annual standard deviations of assets (solid) and equity (dashed). Equity volatility is computed from the equity time series, while asset volatility is implied by the Merton model. Denomination is relative to the value of assets and equity.

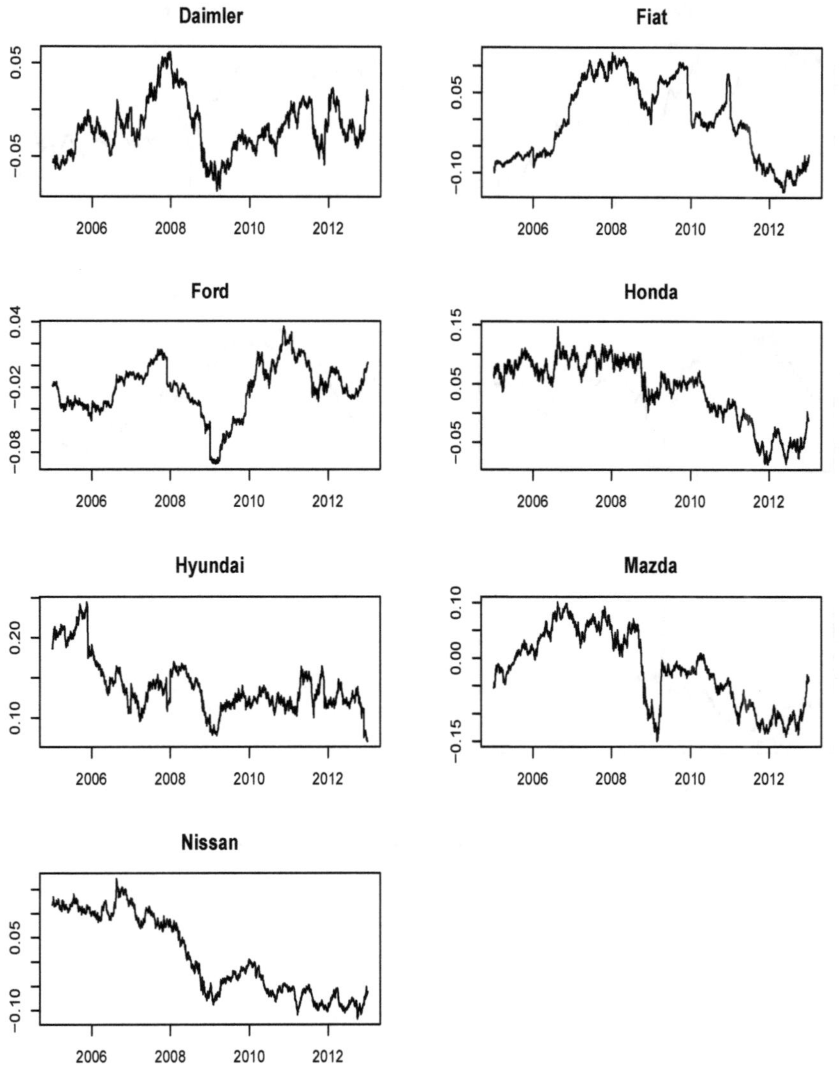
Daimler
0.05
-0.05
Fiat
0.05
-0.10
Ford
0.04
-0.02
-0.08
Honda
0.15
0.05
-0.05
Hyundai
0.20
0.10
Mazda
0.10
0.00
-0.15
Nissan
0.05
-0.10
2006
2008
2010
2012

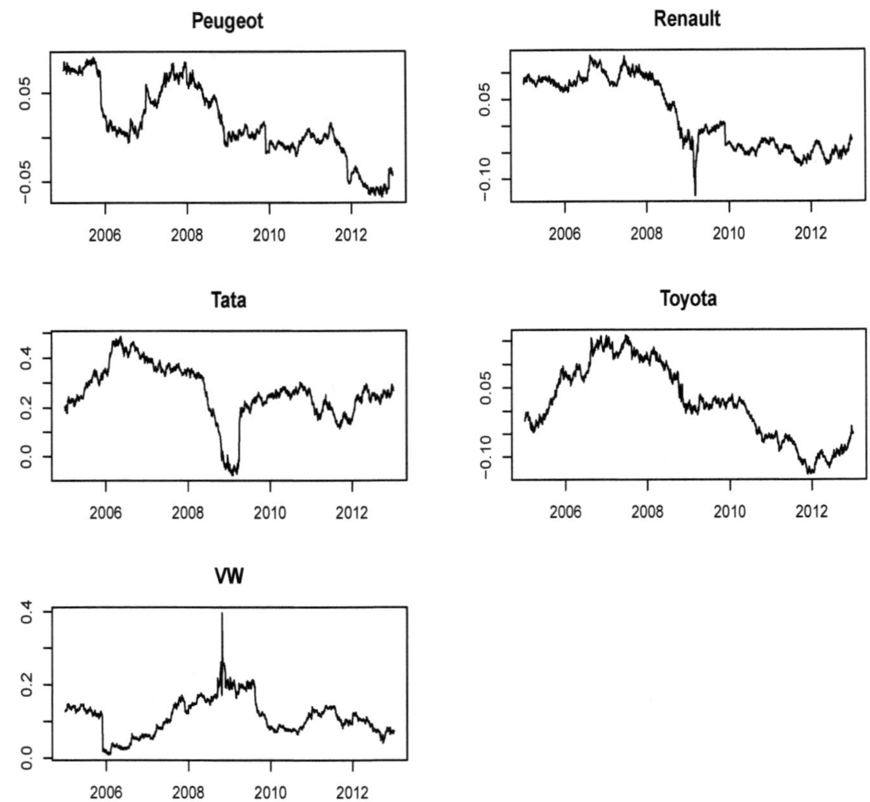

Figure III.6.: **Annual asset growth rate**

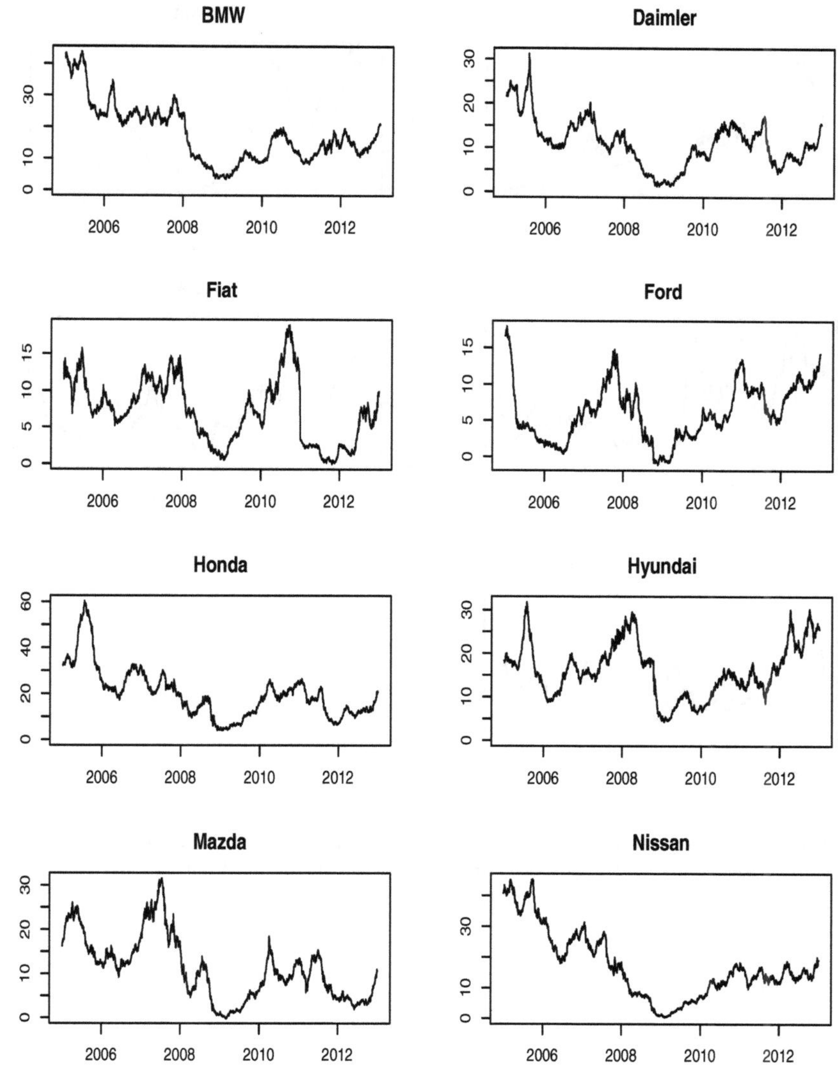
BMW
0
10
30
2006
2008
2010
2012
Daimler
0
10
20
30
2006
2008
2010
2012
Fiat
0
5
10
15
2006
2008
2010
2012
Ford
0
5
10
15
2006
2008
2010
2012
Honda
0
20
40
60
2006
2008
2010
2012
Hyundai
0
10
20
30
2006
2008
2010
2012
Mazda
0
10
20
30
2006
2008
2010
2012
Nissan
0
10
30
2006
2008
2010
2012

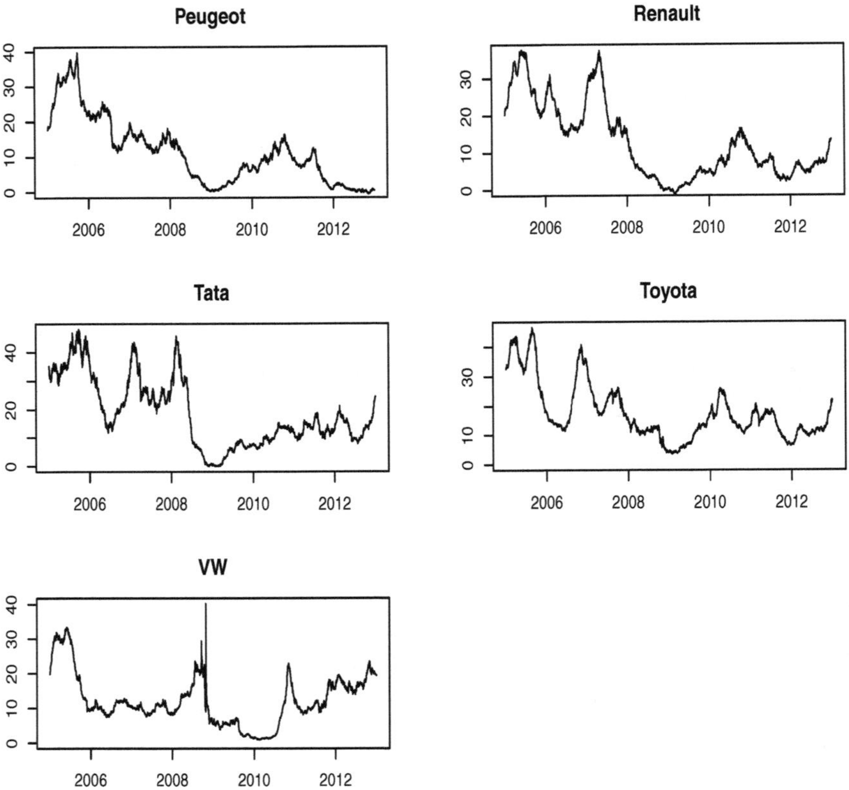

Figure III.7.: **Distance to default:** The figure shows the evolution of the distance between the asset value and the default point at maturity in standard units.

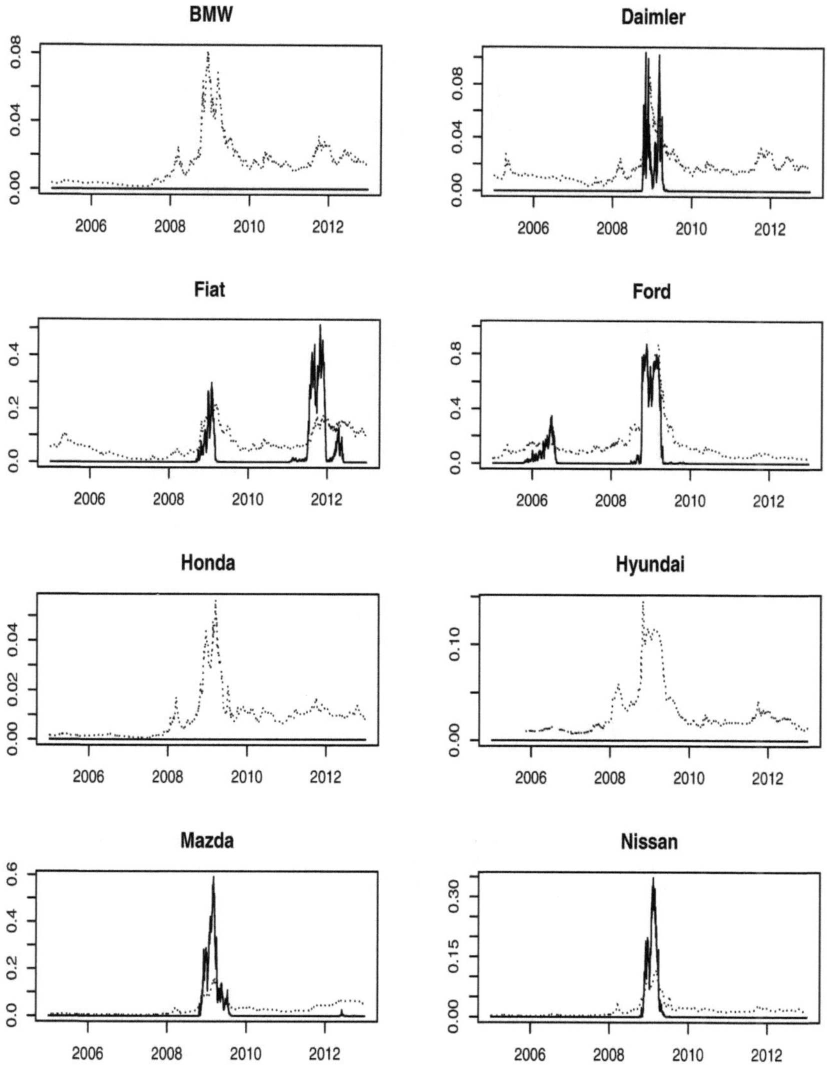
BMW
Daimler
Fiat
Ford
Honda
Hyundai
Mazda
Nissan
2006
2008
2010
2012

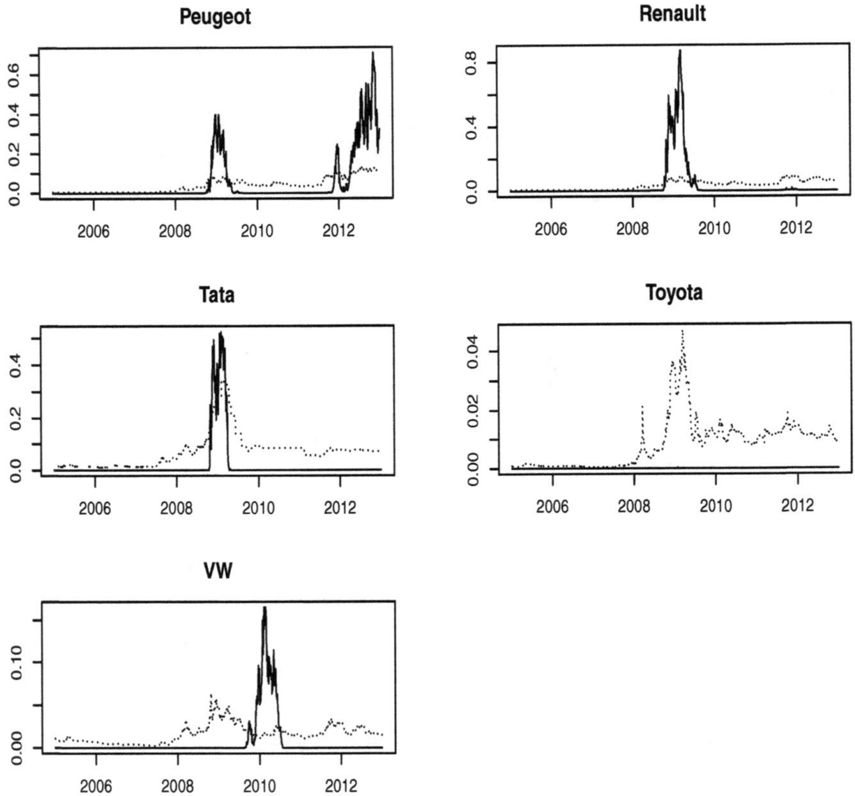

Figure III.8.: **Annual default probabilities:** The figure shows the forecasted default probability obtained from the KMV extension of the Merton model (black) and the market default probability implied by CDS spreads (dotted).

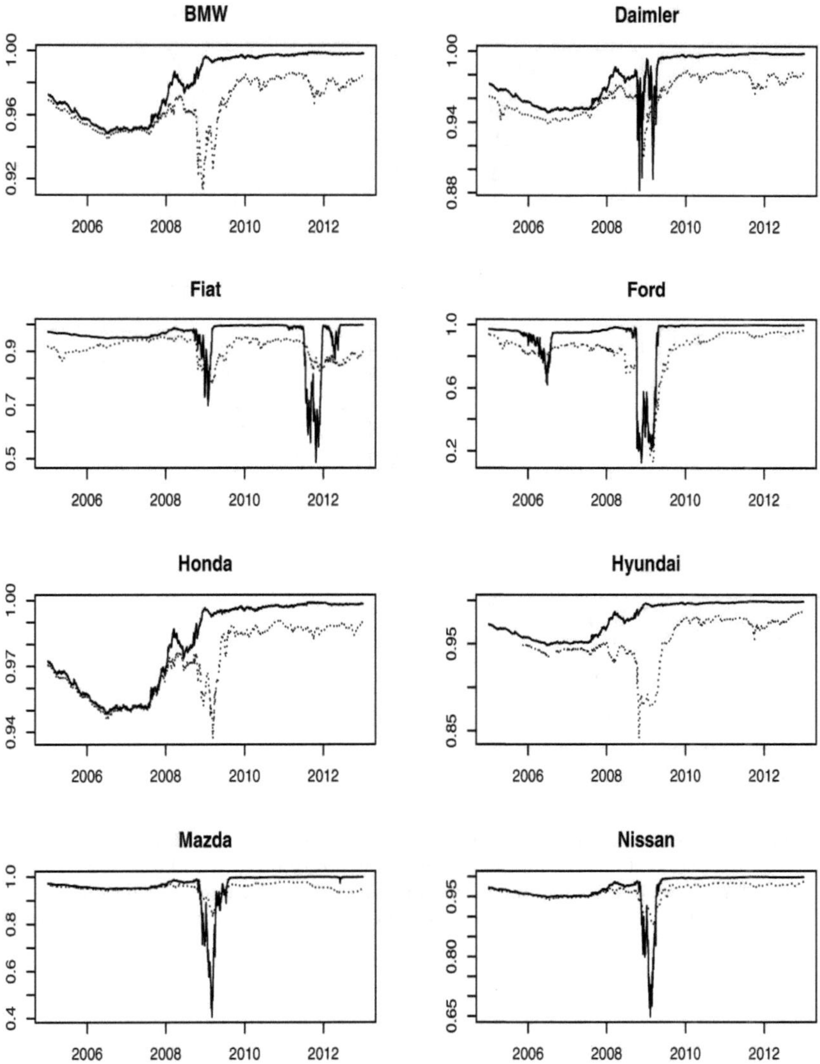
BMW
1.00
0.96
0.92
2006
2008
2010
2012
Daimler
1.00
0.94
0.88
2006
2008
2010
2012
Fiat
0.9
0.7
0.5
2006
2008
2010
2012
Ford
1.0
0.6
0.2
2006
2008
2010
2012
Honda
1.00
0.97
0.94
2006
2008
2010
2012
Hyundai
0.95
0.85
2006
2008
2010
2012
Mazda
1.0
0.8
0.6
0.4
2006
2008
2010
2012
Nissan
0.95
0.80
0.65
2006
2008
2010
2012

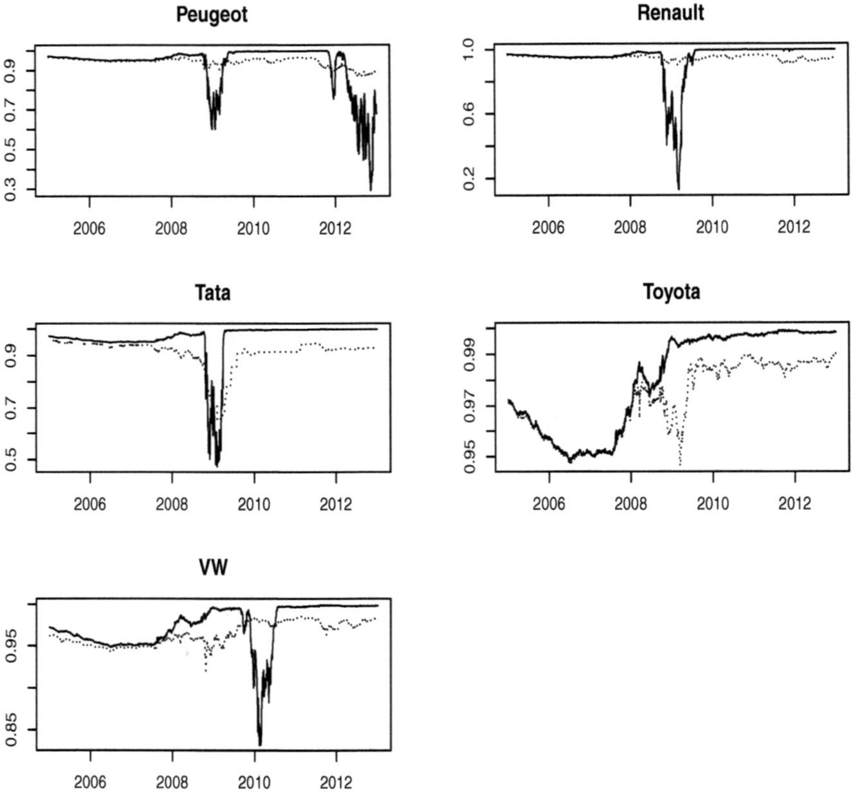

Figure III.9.: **Forecasted price and market price of a standardized bond:** The prices are obtained by discounting the survival probability. The black line gives the forecasted price, while the dotted line gives the market price. The standardized bond has a maturity of one year and offers a repayment of 1 in case of success and 0 in case of failure.

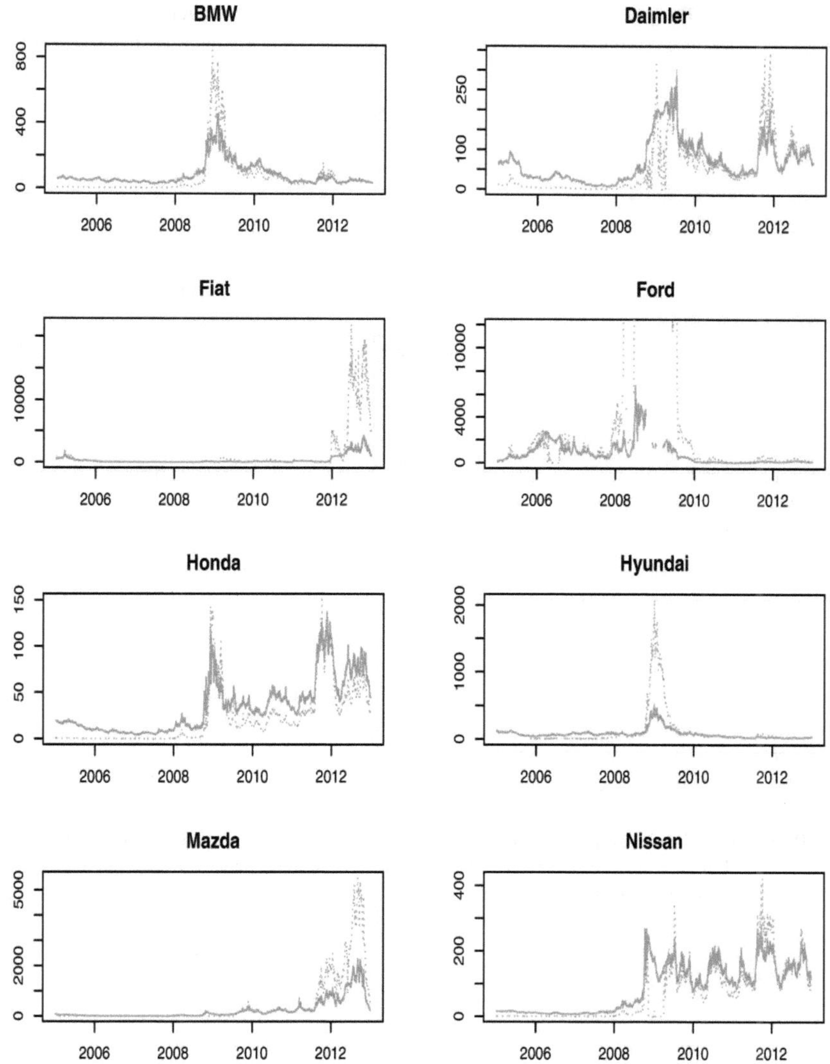
BMW
0
400
800
Daimler
0
100
250
Fiat
0
10000
Ford
0
4000
10000
Honda
0
50
100
150
Hyundai
0
1000
2000
Mazda
0
2000
5000
Nissan
0
200
400
2006
2008
2010
2012

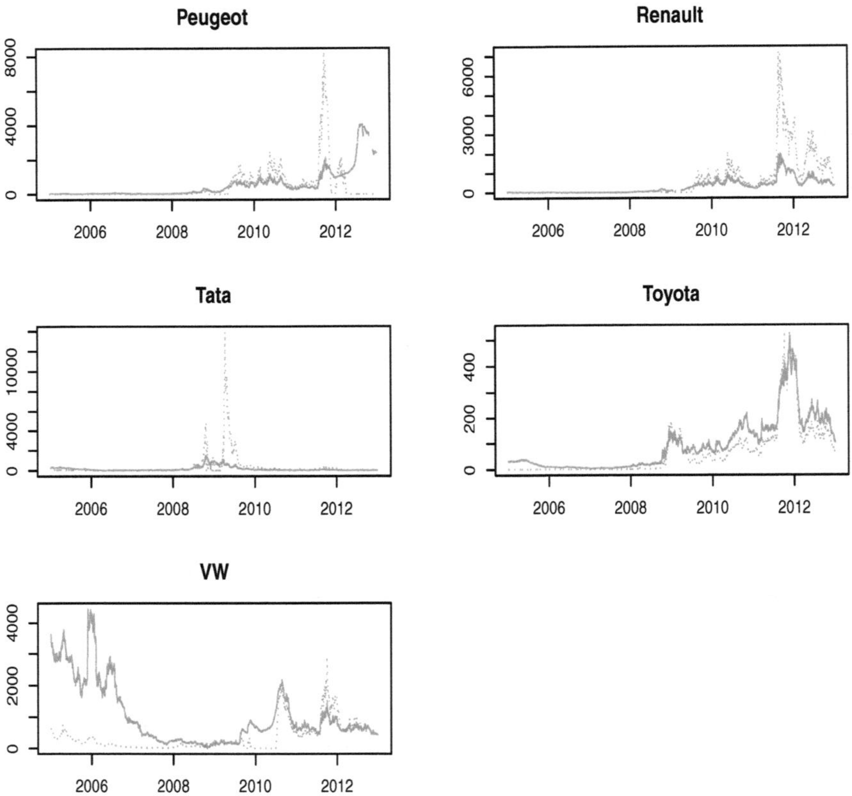

Figure III.10.: **Precision of information:** The figure shows the precision of public information (gray) obtained from (16) and the precision of private information (dotted) obtained from (18).

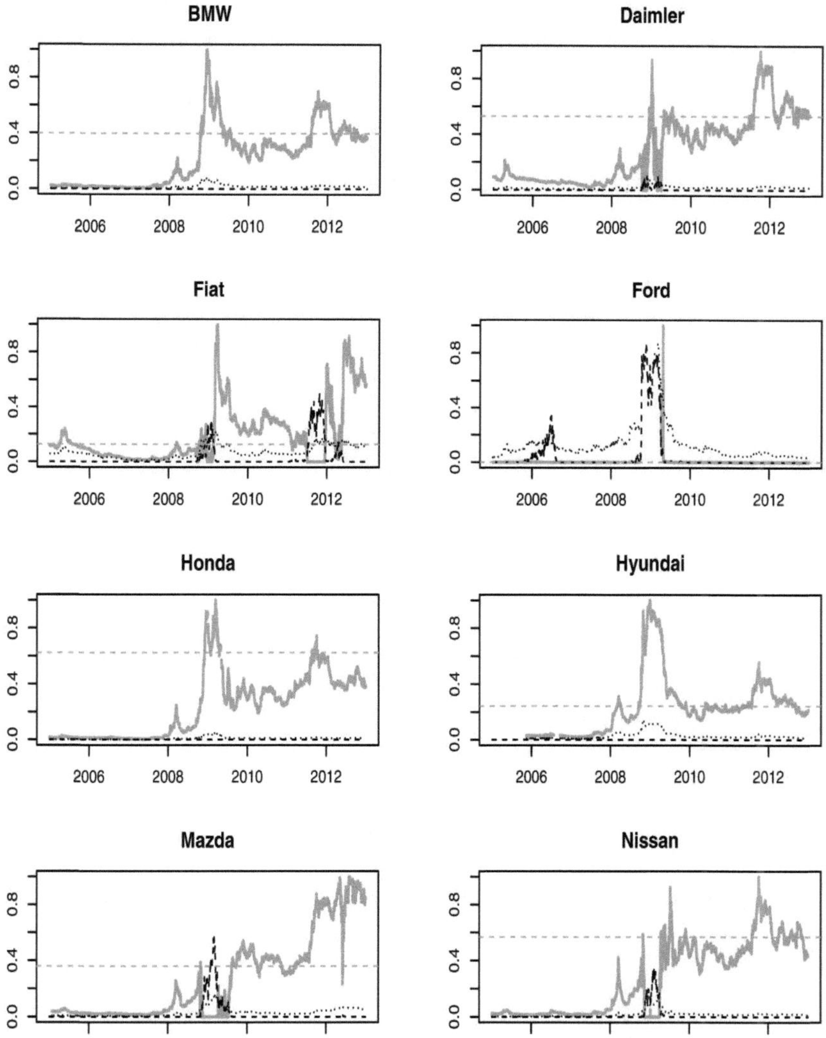
BMW
Daimler
Fiat
Ford
Honda
Hyundai
Mazda
Nissan
0.0
0.4
0.8
2006
2008
2010
2012

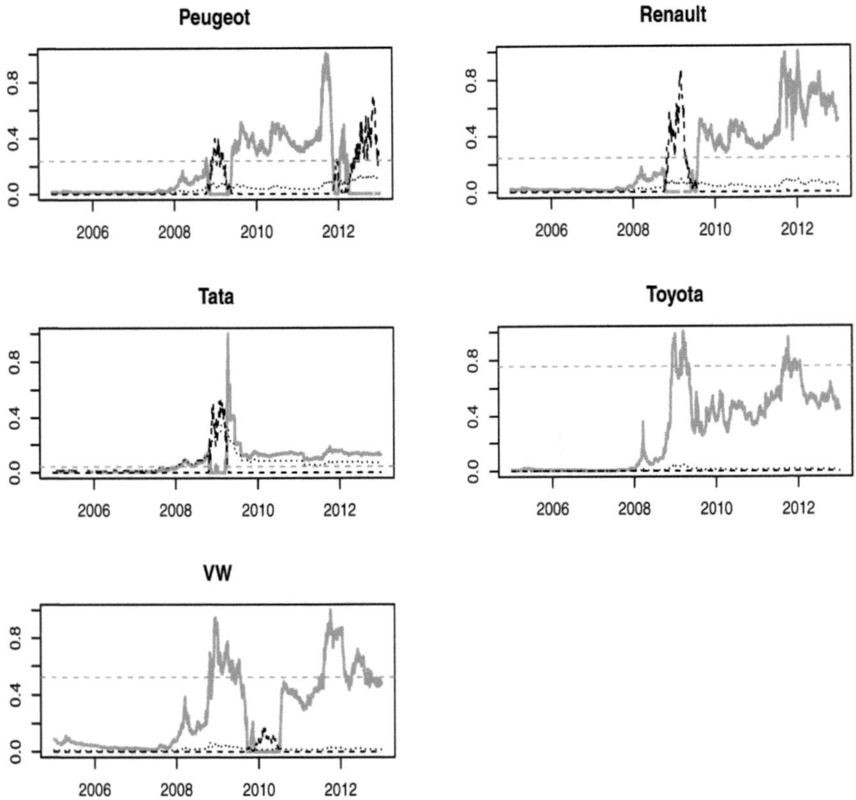

Figure III.11.: **Relative precision and default probabilities:** Shown are the scaled relative precision $\frac{\widetilde{\beta}}{\alpha}$ (gray), the forecasted default probability (dashed black) and the market default probability (dotted black). The dashed horizontal line indicates where $\alpha = \beta$.

Daimler 2008/09

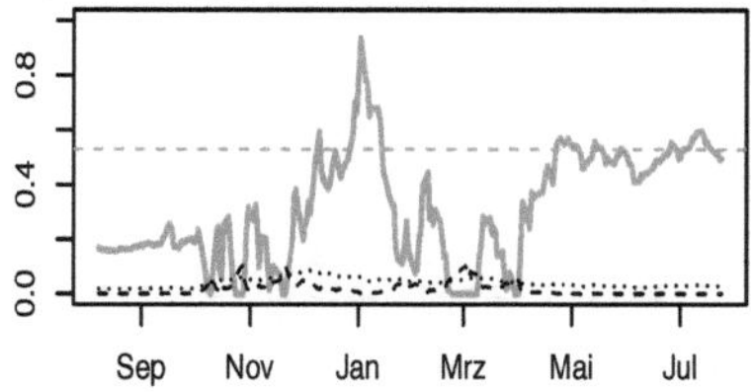

Fiat 2008/09

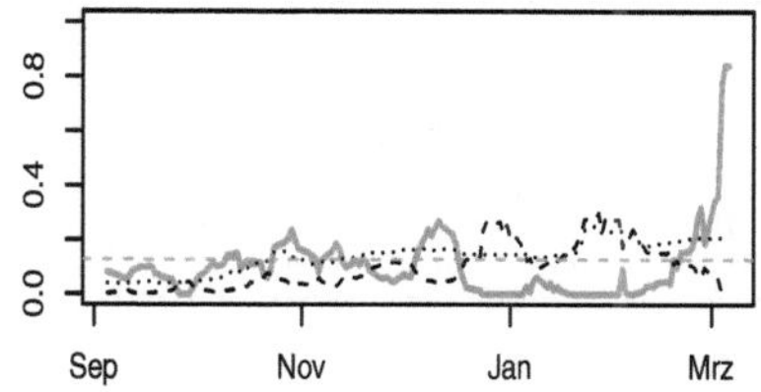

Fiat 2011/12

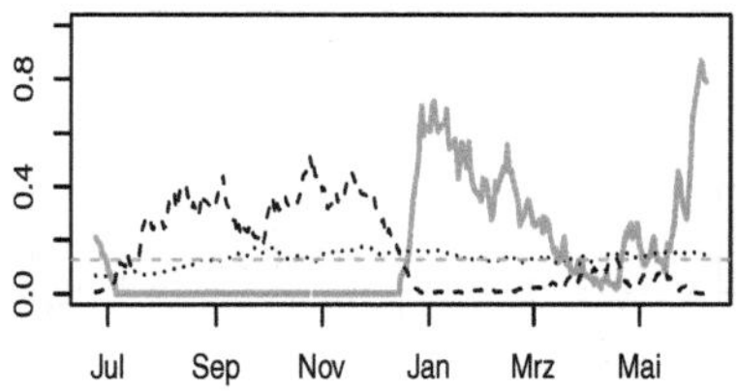

Mazda 2008/09

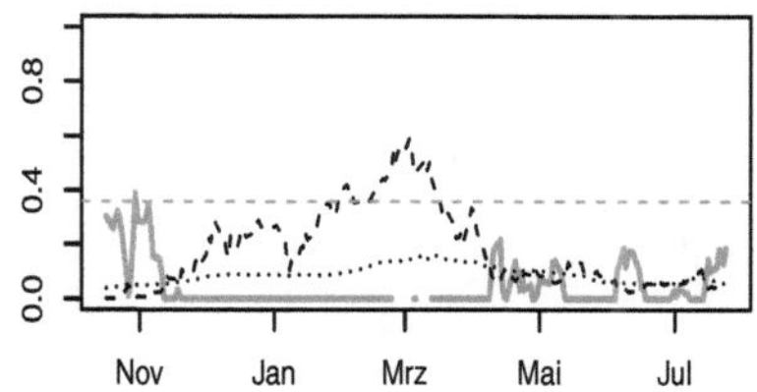

Mazda 2012

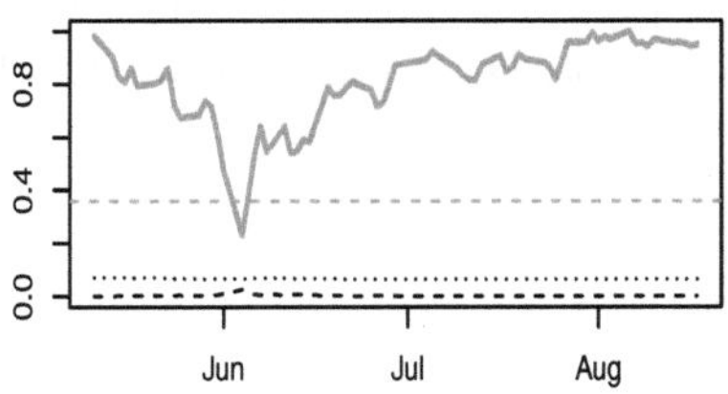

Nissan 2008/09

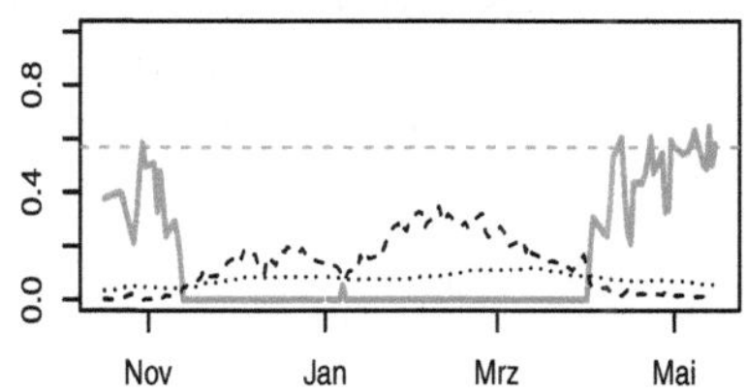

Peugeot 2008/09

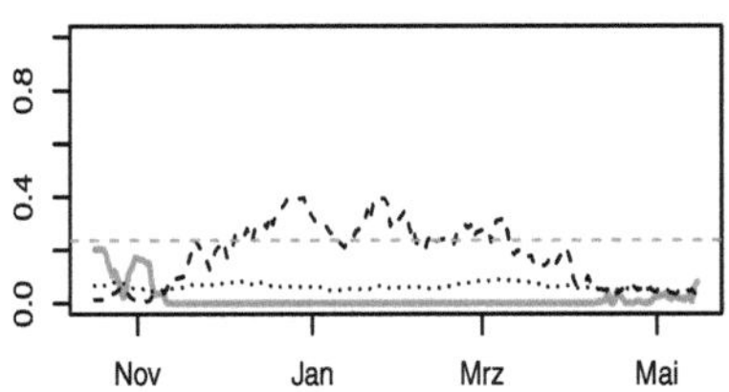

Peugeot 2011/12

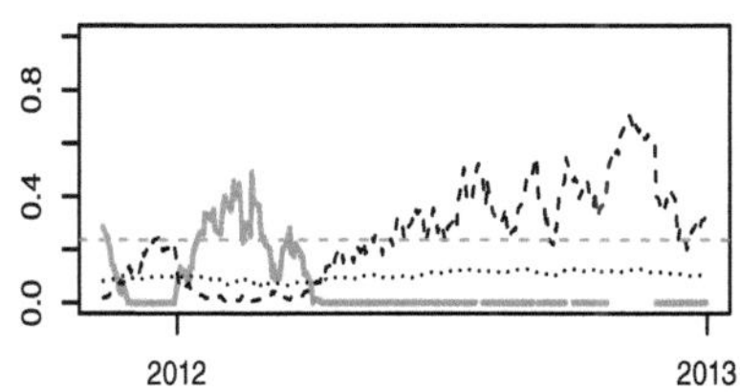

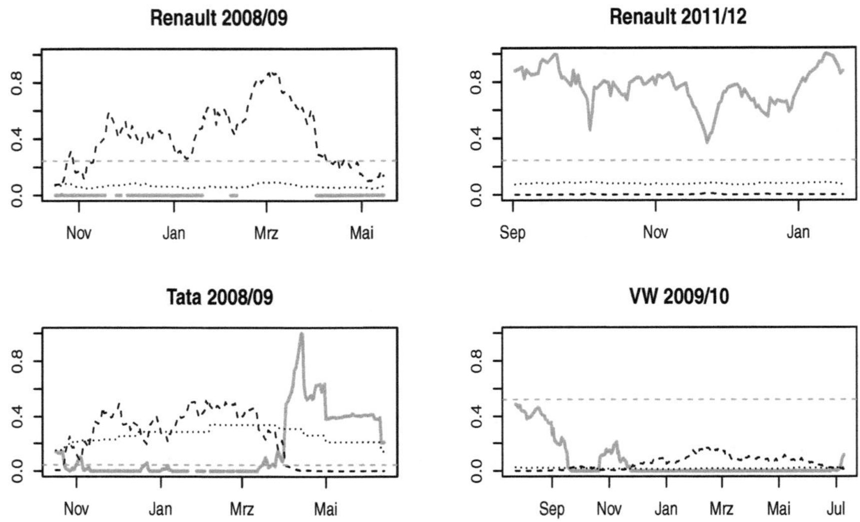

Figure III.12.: **Zoomed in relative precision:** Shown are time spans from figure III.11 when the forecasted default probability (dashed black) rises. Again the scaled relative precision $\widetilde{\frac{\beta}{\alpha}}$ (gray), and the market default probability (dotted black) are plotted. The dashed horizontal line indicates where $\alpha = \beta$.

Bibliography

Angeletos, G.-M., C. Hellwig, and A. Pavan (2006). Signaling in a global game: Coordination and policy traps. *Journal of Political Economy 114*, 452–484.

Angeletos, G.-M., C. Hellwig, and A. Pavan (2007). Dynamic global games of regime change: Learning, multiplicity, and the timing of attacks. *Econometrica 75*, 711–756.

Angeletos, G.-M. and I. Werning (2006). Crises and prices: Information aggregation, multiplicity, and volatility. *The American Economic Review 96*, 1720–1736.

Ashcraft, A., P. Goldsmith-Pinkham, P. Hull, and J. Vickery (2011). Credit ratings and security prices in the subprime MBS market. *American Economic Review: Papers & Proceedings 101*, 115–119.

Atkeson, A. (2001). Comment on rethinking multiple equilibria in macroeconomic modelling. *NBER Macroeconomics Annual 2000 15*, 162–171.

Banerjee, A. V. (1992). A simple model of herd behavior. *The Quaterly Journal of Economics 107*, 797–817.

Bannier, C. E. and F. Heinemann (2005). Optimal transparency and risk-taking to avoid currency crises. *Journal of Institutional and Theretical Economics 161*, 374–391.

Bauer, C. and B. Herz (2013). The dynamics of currency crises–the risk to defend the exchange rate, working paper, mimeo.

Bharath, S. T. and T. Shumway (2008). Forecasting default with the merton distance to default model. *The Review of Financial Studies 21*, 1339–1369.

Bikhchandani, S., D. Hirshleifer, and I. Welch (1992). A theory of fads, fashion, custom, and cultural change as informational cascades. *Journal of Political Economy 100*, 992–1026.

Bolton, P., X. Freixas, and J. Shapiro (2012). The credit ratings game. *Journal of Finance 67*, 85–112.

Boot, A. W. A., T. T. Milbourn, and A. Schmeits (2006). Credit ratings as coordination mechanisms. *The Review of Financial Studies 19*, 81–118.

Cantor, R. and F. Packer (1994). The credit rating industry. *FRBNY Quaterly Review.*

Carlson, M. and G. B. Hale (2006). Rating agencies and sovereign debt rollover. *The B.E. Journal of Macroeconomics 6.*

Chamley, C. (2003). Dynamic speculative attacks. *The American Economic Review 93*, 603–621.

Cornand, C. and F. Heinemann (2008). Optimal degree of public information dissemination. *The Economic Journal 118*, 718–742.

Cornand, C. and F. Heinemann (2009). Speculative attacks with multiple sources of public information. *Scandinavian Journal of Economics 111*, 73–102.

Crosbie, P. and J. Bohn (2003). Modelling default risk. *Moody's KMV Company.*

Crouhy, M., D. Galai, and R. Mark (2000). A comparative analysis of current credit risk models. *Journal of Banking & Finance 24*, 59–117.

Daniëls, T., H. Jager, and F. Klaassen (2011). Currency crises with the threat of an interest rate defence. *Journal of International Economics 85*, 14–24.

Dichev, I. D. and J. D. Piotroski (2001). The long-run stock returns following bond ratings changes. *The Journal of Finance 56*, 173–203.

Edmond, C. (2011). Information manipulation, coordination, and regime change. *NBER Working Papers*, 17395.

European Parliament (2013). Press release: Tougher credit rating rules confirmed by parliament's vote. Plenary Session, 16-01-2013.

Faure-Grimaud, A., E. Peyrache, and L. Quesada (2009). The ownership of ratings. *RAND Journal of Economics 40*, 234–257.

Feichtinger, G. and R. F. Hartl (1986). *Optimale Kontrolle ökonomischer Prozesse.* New York, NY: de Gruyter.

Fisher, I. (1892). *Mathematical Investigation in the Theory of Value and Price. Reprinted: August M. Kelley, New York, 1965.*

Fleming, W. H. and H. M. Soner (2006). *Controlled Markov Processes and Viscosity Solutions* (second ed.). Stochastic Modelling and Applied Probability. New York, NY: Springer Science + Business Media Inc.

Flood, R. P. and P. M. Garber (1984). Collapsing exchange-rate regimes : Some linear examples. *Journal of International Economics 17*(1-2), 1–13.

Goh, J. C. and L. H. Ederington (1993). Is a bond rating downgrade bad news, good news, or no news for stockholders? *The Journal of Finance 48*, 2001–2008.

Griffin, J. M. and D. Y. Tang (2011). Did credit rating agencies make unbiased assumptions on CDOs? *American Economic Review: Papers & Proceedings 101*, 125–130.

Guimaraes, B. (2006). Dynamics of currency crises with asset market frictions. *Journal of International Economics 68*, 141–158.

He, J., J. Qian, and P. E. Strahan (2011). Credit ratings and the evolution of the mortgage-backed securities market. *American Economic Review: Papers & Proceedings 101*(3), 131–135.

Heinemann, F. (2002). Exchange-rate attack as a coordination game: Theory and experimental evidence. *Oxford Review of Economic Policy 18*, 462–478.

Heinemann, F., R. Nagel, and P. Ockenfels (2004). The theory of global games on test: Experimental analysis of coordination games with public and private information. *Econometrica 72*, 1583–1599.

Hörngren, L. and H. Lindberg (1993). The struggle to turn the swedish krona into a hard currency. *Riksbank Working Paper Series* (18).

Hull, J. (2012). Options, futures, and other derivatives. *Prentice Hall.*

Jeanne, O. (1999). Currency crises: A perspective on recent theoretical developments. *CEPR Discussion Papers.*

Jorion, P. and G. Zhang (2007). Information effects of bond rating changes: The role of the rating prior to the announcement. *The Journal of Fixed Income 16*(4), 45–59.

Krugman, P. (1979). A model of balance-of-payments crises. *Journal of Money, Credit and Banking 11*(3), 311–325.

Lindner, A. (2006). Does transparency of central banks produce multiple equilibria on currency markets? *Scandinavian Journal of Economics 108*, 1–14.

Mathis, J., J. McAndrews, and J.-C. Rochet (2009). Rating the raters: Are reputation concerns powerful enough to discipline rating agencies? *Journal of Monetary Economics 56*, 657–674.

Merton, R. C. (1974). On the pricing of corporate debt: The risk structure of interest rates. *The Journal of Finance 29*, 449–470.

Moody's Investors Service Inc. (2013). Ratings definitions. `http://www.moodys.com/ratings-process/Ratings-Definitions/002002`. [Online; accessed 30-April-2013].

Morris, S. and H. S. Shin (1998). Unique equilibrium in a model of self-fulfilling currency attacks. *The American Economic Review 88*, 587–597.

Morris, S. and H. S. Shin (1999). A theory of the onset of currency attacks. In D. V. Pierre-Richard Agnor, Marcus Miller and A. Weber (Eds.), *The Asian Financial Crisis, Causes Contagion and Consequences*, pp. 230–255. Cambridge University Press.

Morris, S. and H. S. Shin (2002). Social value of public information. *The American Economic Review 92*, 1521–1534.

Morris, S. and H. S. Shin (2004). Coordination risk and the price of debt. *European Economic Review 48*, 133–153.

Obstfeld, M. (1994). The logic of currency crises. *Banque de France - Cahiers conomiques et montaires*, 189–213.

Obstfeld, M. (1996). Models of currency crises with self-fulfilling features. *European Economic Review 40*, 1037–1047.

Opp, C. C., M. M. Opp, and M. Harris (2013). Rating agencies in the face of regulation. *Journal of Financial Economics 108*, 46–61.

Skreta, V. and L. Veldkamp (2009). Ratings shopping and asset complexity: A theory of ratings inflation. *Journal of Monetary Economics 56*, 678–695.

Standard & Poor's Financial Services LLC (2010). Default, transition, and recovery: 2009 annual global corporate default study and rating transitions.

Standard & Poor's Financial Services LLC (2013). Standard & poor's ratings services disclaimer. `https://www.mycreditprofile.standardandpoors.com/MCP/html/disclaimers.html`. [Online; accessed 30-April-2013].

Svensson, L. E. O. (2006). Social value of public information: Morris and shin (2002) is actually pro-transparency, not con. *The American Economic Review 96*, 448–452.

Vassalou, M. and Y. Xing (2004). Default risk in equity returns. *The Journal of Finance 59*, 831–868.

Waelde, K. (2008). *Applied Intertemporal Optimization*. Department of Economics, University of Glasgow.

White, L. J. (2010). Markets - the credit rating agencies. *The Journal of Economic Perspectives 24*, 211–226.

Whitman, W. (1865). *Leaves of Grass 1865. Reprinted: Leaves of Grass and other Writings, W. W. Norton & Company, New York, 2002.*

Wicksell, J. G. K. (1898). *Geldzins und Gterpreise. Reprinted: Scientia Verlag Aalen, 1968.*

MIX
Papier aus verantwortungsvollen Quellen
Paper from responsible sources
FSC® C105338

If you have any concerns about our products,
you can contact us on
ProductSafety@springernature.com

In case Publisher is established outside the EU,
the EU authorized representative is:
Springer Nature Customer Service Center GmbH
Europaplatz 3, 69115 Heidelberg, Germany

Printed by Libri Plureos GmbH
in Hamburg, Germany